The Road to Glory

The Inside Story of the Packers' Super Bowl XXXI Championship Season

Written by Bob McGinn

Photographs by
The Milwaukee Journal Sentinel Staff

MILWAUKEE
JOURNAL SENTINEL

MILWAUKEE JOURNAL SENTINEL

Martin Kaiser, *Editor*
George Stanley, *Managing Editor*
Gerry Hinkley, *Deputy Managing Editor*
Garry D. Howard, *Senior Editor/Sports*
Alan King, *Senior Editor/Photo*
Don Walker, *Senior Editor/Enterprise*
Geoff Blaesing, *Senior Editor/Graphics*

Acknowledgements

RESEARCH ASSISTANCE
Martin Kaiser, Garry D. Howard, Don Walker, Tom Pierce, Diane Medinger, Algeria Peoples, Alan King, Geoff Blaesing, Mark Hoffman, Karl Svatek and Benny Sieu, *The Milwaukee Journal Sentinel*; Alan Whitt, Mike Katz, Steve Fecht, Philip K. Webb and Amy Kinsella.

ISBN 1-887761-18-7

COVER AND BOOK DESIGN
Chris Kozlowski

PUBLISHED BY:
AdCraft Sports Marketing
Kaden Tower, 10th Floor
6100 Dutchmans Lane
Louisville, KY 40205
(502) 473-1124

For other sports publications in the AdCraft library, call toll-free (888) 232-7238 or contact our web site at www.sports-mall.com

Karen Sherlock

ABOVE: Upon the team's return to Green Bay, Packers fans lined the downtown streets in an attempt to see their heroes close up.

RIGHT: With the team buses three hours late arriving at Lambeau Field, 61,000 die-hard Packers fans were left to wait in frigid temperatures in the teens.

Photo on Page v by Karen Sherlock

Jack Orton

The entire town of Green Bay turned out to celebrate the Packers' Super Bowl XXXI win in a "Return to Titletown" parade.

Bill Lizdas

Jack Orton

ABOVE: After the team's arrival at Lambeau, Super Bowl MVP Desmond Howard fires up the crowd.

LEFT: Packers coach Mike Holmgren and general manager Ron Wolf hoist the Lombardi Trophy, signifying its return to Green Bay.

Da, da, da-da-da-da, . . . Go-Pack-Go!
Da, da, da-da-da-da, . . . Go-Pack-Go!

If this song — played on a bass guitar and sung by a legion of green-and-gold clad fans at Lambeau Field — is unfamiliar to you, then so are the Green Bay Packers.

Team Wisconsin's theme song may seem as corny as a pair of canvas Converse in the 1990s, but if you've ever watched the Packers play at Lambeau, the song will reverberate in your ears for at least 24 hours — and maybe longer.

Such was the case early in September 1996 when the Packers annihilated the visiting Philadelphia Eagles before a sold-out Lambeau crowd and a national television audience on ABC's Monday Night Football.

It was a victory that I cherished since I left Philadelphia in May 1994 — and The Philadelphia Inquirer — to accept a sports editor's job in Milwaukee.

Many folks back East said coming to the Midwest was not a smart move.

However, after the Packers glorious run to the NFL championship and the incredible work produced by a sports staff that is becoming sharper by the day, I dare to say that my naysayers were wrong.

Completely.

But on this particular Monday evening, as I pointed my gold-colored car back down Interstate 43 toward Milwaukee with Martin Kaiser, my boss, riding shotgun, a conversation ensued looking ahead to Super Bowl XXXI.

Little did Martin (now the paper's editor) and I know at that time that the Packers would be headed to the Big Easy, in search of the first Super Bowl title for the franchise since the Vince Lombardi-led Packers crushed the Oakland Raiders, 33-14, in Miami in 1967.

Almost 30 years later, the Packers' success has kept the sports department at The Journal Sentinel quite busy.

In January it has made life, well, hell for

Bob McGinn

Bob McGinn, the author of this book.

McGinn doesn't look like Brett Favre, the two-time reigning MVP of the National Football League and the Packers' star quarterback.

Not at all.

First off, McGinn wears glasses that make his eyes seem bigger than they really are; doesn't have the body to take the pounding of a professional quarterback; and I doubt very seriously if he can wing a football like the leader of the Pack.

On the other hand, Favre can't write and report like McGinn.

Not at all.

Still, it has been McGinn's pleasure, I'm sure, to cover the Packers like no other NFL beat writer in America.

As you sit back and peruse this wonderful compilation of his work — including every game story from Green Bay's memorable 1996 season — remember that this is a young man who lives near Green Bay, has covered the team for many years, and, as a reporter, asks questions that many are just plain afraid to ask.

McGinn confronts the people behind the stories, uses his myriad of sources to get the

inside scoop on the team to which he is assigned and is there every day to back up what he writes in The Journal Sentinel.

Inside the press room after the Packers crushed the Eagles, 39-13, on that beautiful Monday evening last September, I saw McGinn tapping lightly on a door. Sitting in that private box was Packers general manager Ron Wolf, who always made himself available to McGinn after every game. I watched McGinn work. He was smooth. Fast. And he turned in a story that put Green Bay's victory in perspective. It is that kind of hard work and fast feet that has helped him become a top-shelf writer.

As sports editor, it is my charge to ensure that this newspaper gets the very best from its sports writers. In the case of Mr. McGinn, however, I don't have to do much at all.

Really.

During the week leading up to the Packers' fantastic finish, The Journal Sentinel published a Super Bowl special section each day in addition to the regular sports section. The photo department, led by senior editor Alan King, was a huge part of the newspaper's success, producing top-quality work on a daily basis — much of which you will find in this book.

McGinn was also a major part of that production. And he still had to write three special pieces for this book.

Luck, my mother Ann Boone Howard told me so often as I grew up in the South Bronx, is the residue of hard work. And I have seen few writers work as hard as McGinn.

After you finish reading this book, I'm sure you'll agree with my assessment:

Bob McGinn can bring the heat.

Please, do enjoy!

Garry D. Howard
Senior Editor/Sports
Milwaukee Journal Sentinel

While Reggie White leads the Packers in the locker room, Mike Holmgren is in control at game time.

Dynamic Duo Puts Packers Back on Top

GREEN BAY — Twenty-five years of waiting and finally the Green Bay Packers found everything they had ever wanted in Ron Wolf.

Introduced as the Packers' executive vice president and general manager shortly after lunch on Wednesday, Nov. 27, 1991, Wolf flew back to Long Island later that same afternoon to clear out his office with the New York Jets.

Four days later, Wolf hurried to Atlanta for the Green Bay Packers' game against the Falcons. Unlike so many others, the first day on the job for Wolf was a time for action, not orientation.

Before the game, Wolf excused himself from Packers president Bob Harlan and walked onto the field at Atlanta-Fulton County Stadium. Amid the greetings and handshakes, Wolf was on a mission to observe the Falcons' third-string quarterback, a raw but rifle-armed rookie named Brett Favre.

Favre had lasted until the 33rd selection in April 1991 but Wolf personally rated him the No.1 player in the entire draft. Wolf just wanted to observe Favre in warmups for a few minutes to confirm his pre-draft evaluation.

"He came back up to the press box and said he wanted to trade for Brett Favre," Harlan recalled. And the fateful trade of a first-round draft choice for Favre would take place Feb. 11, 1992.

Four weeks later, Wolf interviewed San Francisco 49ers offensive coordinator Mike Holmgren on a Sunday in the club's nearly deserted administrative building. Again, his mind was made up almost instantly.

"Very briefly into the interview I knew there wasn't any sense for me to go any further," Wolf said on Jan. 11, 1992, the day Holmgren was named coach. "It was the mesh between two people. I felt like I had known Mike pretty near all my life. Here was a gentleman I felt I could work with."

Thus, the Packers' inexorable climb from the 4-12 depths and eight games behind the division-winning Detroit Lions in 1991 to the 13-3 heights and the Super Bowl in 1996. For a quarter century the Packers almost were an anachronism, road kill on someone else's drive to the top. After the five-year plan of Wolf and Holmgren reached fruition the Packers themselves were at the summit.

"I don't know if the people appreciate the jump the Packers franchise has taken under Ron Wolf and Mike Holmgren," Harlan said late in the season as the

Packers rode to glory. "I think they are the best in the league."

No organization in the league could even approach Green Bay in talent at the three most vital positions: General manager, coach and quarterback.

When the general manager worked ungodly hours on personnel and made shrewd move after shrewd move, when the coach proved himself a born leader with the offensive flair and reasonable approach to discipline as the great coaches, and when the quarterback accepted the coach's constructive criticism and developed himself into a two-time Most Valuable Player, it was just a matter of time before Green Bay would become Titletown again three decades after Lombardi.

Rebuilding?

It was more than that.

When Wolf and Holmgren went to work in the winter of 1992, they were inheriting a truly bad football team from Lindy Infante. For the first time in 15 years the Packers hadn't defeated an opponent that finished with a winning record, and no Packer had made the Pro Bowl.

But even more daunting was the perception among some football people, especially with unrestricted free agency on the horizon, that it would be a cold day in hell before another championship was won by the National Football League's smallest city.

"I remember in the mid-1980s, everybody would say to me at league meetings, 'Boy, you better hope free agency never comes. It will kill you guys,'" Harlan once said. "And I can't say we didn't wonder if it would kill us."

Green Bay was regarded by some players and coaches as the dregs of the league, the NFL's Siberia. The Packers had been treated with condescension, even ridicule, during their almost comically misguided steps to right their sinking ship.

Ron Wolf, the architect of the NFC champion Packers, celebrates with some of the players after beating Carolina for the NFC title.

Wolf, however, had no ties to Green Bay or Wisconsin. Neither did Holmgren. In fact, each had spent most of their lives in California.

While the Packers had been foundering for a generation, Wolf was winning two Super Bowl rings with the Raiders and Holmgren a pair with the 49ers.

Certainly, each man paid homage to the Packers' tradition as one of the NFL's charter teams. Neither man, however, was encumbered by the Glory Years because they had established themselves as proven winners somewhere else.

From the onset their turf was clearly marked out. As Holmgren's boss, Wolf would have final say on all personnel decisions but only after he agreed to consult with Holmgren every step of their journey.

Just as Holmgren informed Wolf that he had little interest in performing a scout's daily grunt work, Wolf told Holmgren that he wouldn't coach the team from the press box as his mentor, Al Davis, had done with the Raiders.

"There haven't been many disagreements because there's a mutual respect for each other," Wolf said. "I think he's an honest, honorable person. His M.O. is to make sure we field the best possible team we can field. He doesn't worry about change, which is so important."

Thus, Wolf is able to conduct himself almost like the mad professor of the film room, pushing his expanded staff of scouts in a never-sending search for players that leaves no stone or league unturned. And when his unyielding work ethic results in the possibility of trade or transaction, Wolf makes sure to call Holmgren first before any action is taken.

"He's a wild man," Holmgren said last summer after Wolf consummated one of his 49 trades in their five years together. "Do you know how many deals I've said no to? Every day there's a couple, three things. Every day."

When Reggie White (hugging Holmgren) was signed in 1993, the goal was to win a NFL championship.

There might be only one or two other general managers in the NFL who operate as Wolf does, scouting players on campus Tuesday through Friday or Saturday every week from September until mid-November, studying tapes of players in the league by himself and in conjunction with his three full-time pro scouts, setting up the draft board and negotiating selected contracts.

Wolf might take one or two weeks of vacation each summer, but seldom does a day pass that he isn't calling the office. One personnel director cited Wolf's diligence in working at personnel 365 days a year as one of the edges that the Packers have in a dog-eat-dog industry.

Holmgren cut his professional teeth under Bill Walsh, under whom he became accustomed to the quest for perfection, the need for being cold and impersonal at times, and the importance of being at least

experience has never been an issue with his players. He coached Joe Montana and Steve Young to brilliance and his ability to direct the West Coast offense with dynamic results goes without saying.

Little or nothing in or around the team gets by Holmgren. He despises taunting, show-boating and cheap shots. Control is very much a priority with him.

Although Holmgren's leash is tight, and his temper behind closed doors is legendary, he isn't so inflexible that his methods have had a harmful effect on the creative or athletic gifts of his players.

"They say he's a player's coach, and he is," Packers safety Eugene Robinson said. "He's like Mr. Dad. But even when you're winning he cuts at you a little bit to make sure you know you're not perfect."

His teams, much more physical than Infante's ever were, still have been among the league leaders in fewest turnovers and penalties. The offensive system has been tested true over time, it is taught by a veteran staff of coaches, and the emphasis is on minimizing mental mistakes.

As Walsh did before him, Holmgren's practices are heavy on tempo and execution and light on contact. One reason why the Packers have flourished, not perished, in free agency is the universal appeal among players on how they practice in Green Bay.

"He treats people like men," Packers backup quarterback Jim McMahon said. "Training camp here ... I just loved it. I think if our guys (in Chicago) had been to training camp like this every year they'd still be playing."

In 1992, Holmgren's decision to make Green Bay the first team in league history to have two black coordinators, Sherman Lewis on offense and Ray Rhodes on defense, was hailed as a visionary step throughout the NFL. He would lose Rhodes to the 49ers two years later, but the quick hiring of Fritz

receptive to change.

After their pre-draft meetings in the spring, Holmgren is conversant on about the top 150 players. He reads all the scouting reports and listens to everything that is said.

"Ultimately, Ron and I go into one of our offices and make the call," Holmgren said. "As long as we can take the emotion out of it, and he says that to me a lot, most every call we make we can live with."

Whereas Holmgren marvels at Wolf's near photographic recall of players and overall scouting acumen, Wolf seems equally as impressed by the way in which Holmgren teaches quarterbacks, calls plays, develops players, and is able to foster unselfishness and unity in the era of liberal player movement.

Holmgren's quarterbacking career dead-ended early at the University of Southern California but his lack of NFL

Shurmur to run the defense more than sufficed as damage control.

Again, continuity was served. Shurmur agreed to learn Rhodes' successful defensive system and then implement it with variations to ease the burden on the players.

While up to one-third of the league's coaches seem to be fired every year, the Packers' edge in stability becomes greater and greater.

They have run the same offense for five years, the same defense for five years, and the special teams have been coordinated for five years by the same assistant coach, Nolan Cromwell.

When it comes time to finding players for the system, the Packers operate almost at an unfair advantage. Wolf and Holmgren possess unparalleled job security and after so much time they know exactly what type of players they need to make the system work.

For instance, wide receivers need size and ability to run after the catch, tight ends must be able to catch, offensive linemen should be athletic, quarterbacks must be mobile and smart, running backs need good hands, size is vital for defensive linemen, the linebackers should be fast and the cornerbacks, in the wake of the Terrell Buckley fiasco, definitely can't be diminutive.

Buckley isn't the only skeleton rattling around in the Wolf-Holmgren closet. The early attempts to locate a running back failed, Bryce Paup was needlessly lost in free agency, and the trade-up for George Teague in the first round of 1993 didn't pan out.

Unlike some teams, though, the Packers seldom exacerbate their errors by sticking with players. Buckley and Teague were given three years before they were replaced by Craig Newsome and Robinson, key components of what

might have been the NFL's finest secondary in 1996.

Few, if any, personnel moves in the last 10 to 15 years can compare in impact with the trade for Favre. But the free-agent pursuit and subsequent signing of Reggie White in April 1993 might have been as significant because of what it meant for Green Bay's image among players, particularly premier black players, across the league.

Plus, White became the leader of all leaders in the locker room.

Neither Wolf nor Holmgren saw any

Holmgren charts the Packers' opening 15 plays of every game.

need to accept no for an answer when everyone in the league kept telling them the Packers had no shot at White.

Moreover, they refused to believe that Lambeau Field, so hospitable for visitors during the coaching tenures of Forrest Gregg and Infante, couldn't become one of the tougher places to play in the NFL.

Bucking the odds. Smashing the stereotypes. Turning negatives into positives.

Together, Ron Wolf and Mike Holmgren built a futile franchise into a Super Bowl champion.

Mike Holmgren's Packers have won 28 of 29 games at Lambeau Field.

The Season

Stars of the game: Brett Favre congratulates LeRoy Butler on his second interception of the game. Favre jumpstarted his MVP season with a fourtouchdown performance.

Game 1

Green Bay	10	14	10	0	34
Tampa Bay	0	3	0	0	3

Packers' season starts in style

TAMPA, FLA. — The Road to New Orleans will be eminently more arduous than this. But did the Green Bay Packers ever accelerate off the line Sunday.

Extracting revenge for a costly defeat in this stadium last December and striking a blow for themselves as a team to be reckoned with in the Super Bowl race, the Packers destroyed the Tampa Bay Buccaneers, 34-3, before 54,102 at Houlihan's Stadium.

It was the largest margin of victory in an opening regular-season game for the Packers since Vince Lombardi's 1965 team debuted with a 41-9 victory in Pittsburgh. And it also turned Tony Dungy's baptismal as Buccaneers coach into a nightmare.

"It's one small step," Packers general manager Ron Wolf said, mindful of the Buccaneers' streak of 13 consecutive losing seasons. "But it's a large step for us because it's a division opponent and on the road."

There were elements of inherent dangers for the Packers despite the opponent.

The Buccaneers should have been emotionally ready to play for Dungy, long regarded as a player's coach during his years as a NFL assistant.

With the mercury at 86 degrees and the humidity at 65%, the chances for a premature wilt was a threat, especially with the Packers in dark jerseys.

"This guy (Dungy) is a very good coach

The Packers' pass rush was relentless, knocking heads — and helmets — around most of the afternoon. In this case Buccaneer offensive lineman Jim Pyne was the victim.

here," Wolf said.

But in the end, it was the same old Buccaneers.

On offense, Green Bay coach Mike Holmgren's inspired play-calling completely baffled Dungy, his longtime defensive adversary.

Once Dungy declared his intentions to roll coverages toward Robert Brooks and, at times, Antonio Freeman, Holmgren went for the jugular by sending tight ends Keith Jackson and Mark Chmura into one-on-one matchups against linebackers. Jackson had three first-half touchdown receptions of 1, 4 and 51 yards and finished with five receptions for 76 yards.

On defense, the Packers forced six turnovers — one more than in any game coached by Holmgren, and the club's high since it forced eight against Tampa Bay in the same stadium in mid-1991 — to accomplish precisely what defensive coordinator Fritz Shurmur had emphasized since the first day of the first minicamp.

Last year, the Packers didn't get their sixth takeaway until the seventh game and finished 30th and last in turnovers.

"We got great jumps on the ball," Shurmur said. "I've never seen a guy go up in the air before like LeRoy (Butler) did."

Butler, seeing the ball better since his late-July decision to wear contact lenses, had two of the four interceptions against overmatched Tampa Bay quarterback Trent Dilfer. Dungy patiently tried to run the ball early, but without holdout 1,000-yard rusher Errict Rhett, his motley collection of ball carriers was no match for Green Bay's defense.

Wolf and Shurmur were quick to acknowledge that this wasn't much of a challenge for the defense. "We caught them a little bit early in the implementation of their system," Shurmur said.

Not to be outdone, the special teams also were exceptional in taking game-

Photo on Pages 19-20 by Jeffrey Phelps

breaking rookie returner Nilo Silvan totally out of the contest. Craig Hentrich aver-
aged 44.5 yards on five punts and kicked
off high and long.

By comparison, it was a play that the
Buccaneers failed to make on special teams

that turned what had been a fairly competitive game into a rout.

Late in the second quarter, with the
Packers leading, 10-3, Chris Jacke kicked a
27-yard field goal on fourth-and-2. On the
play, Buccaneers rookie defensive end

Regan Upshaw was penalized for grabbing
tackle Earl Dotson so that a trailing
defender could leap through the opening
and block the kick.

Holmgren took a poll of his coaches.
They decided to take the three points off

Mark Hoffman

the board.

On the next play, Packers quarterback Brett Favre hit Jackson in the end zone for a touchdown and it was 17-3, not 13-3. And when the Buccaneers went three-and-out and punted, Favre found Jackson meandering by himself behind the deflated Tampa Bay secondary for a 51-yard touchdown with 39 seconds left in the half.

Trailing 24-3, the Buccaneers were finished.

Keith Jackson's third touchdown of the day was a 51-yarder, one of his five catches for 76 yards.

Potent, Powerful and in Prime Time

GREEN BAY — The Green Bay Packers' first Monday night home game in a decade turned into a sheer, unadulterated mismatch before a joyously appreciative throng in the NFL's smallest city.

Mixing Brett Favre's sensational passing with brutally effective running, the Packers routed the Philadelphia Eagles, 39-13, before a record Lambeau Field crowd of 60,666.

"It was just an unbelievably great win for us," Packers coach Mike Holmgren said. "We were ready to play and turnovers ... turnovers again. We're getting turnovers this year. We didn't get any last year."

Prepared for an intense war of wits with two of his former assistants, Eagles coach Ray Rhodes and offensive coordinator Jon Gruden, Holmgren's team dominated in every phase of play.

"You have to be very impressed with the play of every unit," Packers general manager Ron Wolf said. "Offense. Defense. Special teams. Our team really responded."

Green Bay has won 19 of its last 20 regular-season and playoff games in Lambeau Field and is tied with surprising Minnesota atop the NFL Central.

Robert Brooks has a flock of Eagles in pursuit as he scores on a 25-yard reception from Brett Favre in the first quarter.

Moreover, the Packers, annually a chronic slow starter, have started a season 2-0 for the first time since 1982.

"Playing here really helps us," Holmgren said. "Lambeau Field now is really, really a great home-field advantage."

Are the Packers a Super Bowl team after crushing the Eagles, a 10-6 club last year, and the wily Rhodes?

"Oh, that's way too early," Wolf said. "What we have to do is take care of our own business, our own division. But this is a conference game so it's very important."

"I don't know if they are or not," said John Wooten, the Eagles' director of college scouting. "Green Bay's a good football team. Very good. But to make the kind of mistakes we made, you're going to get beat."

Favre was at his improvisational finest after an ugly start, finishing with 17 completions in 31 attempts for 261 yards and three scores.

Favre was wild high at the onset, whipping five consecutive incompletions without much pressure from the Eagles. But then the six-year veteran went on a tear, finishing the first half 14-for-27 for 222 yards and two touchdowns.

Dancing away from the rush like a

Linebacker George Koonce picks off a pass in the first quarter, one of three interceptions the Packers had in the game.

matador with a cape. Putting perfect touch and trajectory on deep passes. Finding open receivers when the play seemed pointless.

"Unbelievable," said Rick Spielman, the Detroit Lions' assistant director of pro personnel who was scouting the Packers for the second straight week. "Favre is unconscious right now. The way he improvises and finds the open receiver ... he's the best quarterback overall in the league right now. No one comes close to him."

Robert Brooks caught four passes for 116 yards in the first half, including touch-

Safety LeRoy Butler takes flight to bring down Eagles quarterback Rodney Peete in the Packers' first Monday Night Football appearance at Lambeau Field in 10 years.

Jeffrey Phelps

Tom Lynn

A familiar sight: Brett Favre hugs Robert Brooks after throwing a third quarter touchdown pass to the star receiver.

down receptions of 25 and 20 yards. On the final play of the half, Don Beebe dropped a deflected Hail Mary pass that would have been a 51-yard touchdown.

As it was, the Packers went to the locker room ahead, 30-7.

"I was at the Tampa game and the Packers looked even better tonight against a better football team," Spielman said. "You can't make a mistake against the Packers. They know how to take advantage."

The Eagles (1-1) turned the ball over three times in the first quarter. Those takeaways led to Green Bay's first 13 points and the rout was on.

As the offensive explosion unfolded, the noise from the sellout crowd became louder and louder and louder.

"It's like a playoff atmosphere here

Reggie White (92) directs a post-game prayer with players from both teams following the 39-13 blowout of Philadelphia.

tonight," Spielman said.

After his 0-for-5 start, Favre caught fire after Sean Jones stripped the ball from Ricky Watters at the Green Bay 43. The Eagles had 131 yards in the first half, with 62 coming on a pass and lateral from quarterback Rodney Peete to Chris T. Jones. The lateral to Irving Fryar gained the final 33 yards and set up the Eagles' touchdown by Watters.

In the final 18 minutes of the first half, Favre passed 20 yards to Mark Chmura, 25 and a touchdown to Brooks, 38 to Brooks, 33 to Brooks, 21 to Antonio Freeman and 20 and another touchdown to Brooks.

The Eagles' offense went nowhere. Peete's first pass was intercepted by Doug Evans, Craig Newsome broke up a third-down pass to force a punt on their second possession, and Watters' fumble ruined their third series. Santana Dotson batted a pass by Peete and linebacker George Koonce intercepted on Philadelphia's fourth possession.

The Packers also hurt the Eagles with a power ground game behind fullback William Henderson's booming lead blocks. In the third quarter, the Packers ran on seven straight plays to close out the third quarter, gaining 35 yards.

Dorsey Levens gained 14 on third-and-5 to open the fourth quarter. Three more runs in a row — extending the unprecedented string to 11 in the Holmgren era — set up fourth-and-goal at the 3.

But the concerted push ended when Mike Arthur's snap sailed over holder Craig Hentrich's head, wiping out Chris Jacke's chance for a fourth field goal.

Asked if the Packers were the NFL's best team, Favre said, "I don't want to go that far. We're executing. A lot of good things have been said about us but that won't get it done. We're just playing well right now."

The Packers have outscored their first two opponents, 73-16.

| San Diego | 3 | 0 | 0 | 7 | 10 |
| Green Bay | 7 | 14 | 7 | 14 | 42 |

A 3-0 Start Gives Packers a Charge

GREEN BAY — For most of the Mike Holmgren era, the Green Bay Packers were incapable of pounding the ball or being truly dominant with the pass rush.

Finesse football might be too simple a label, but in many ways it was an apt description for the last four seasons in Green Bay.

These Packers, though, are forging their own identity, one that could be much different from that of their most recent predecessors.

Against a Bobby Ross-coached team that built its reputation by beating up opponents, Green Bay proved for a third consecutive week that power is back in vogue. It manhandled the San Diego Chargers, 42-10, Sunday before 60,584 at Lambeau Field.

"Everybody talks about the West Coast offense, but they're a physical football team," Billy Devaney, the Chargers' director of player personnel, said about the Packers. "I don't know what the story was in the past because we don't play them, but right now they're both a skillful and physical team."

The 32-point margin represented the worst defeat for San Diego since 1988, or four years before Ross brought toughness to a soft operation. Some Chargers were comparing this destruction to their 49-26 loss to San Francisco in Super Bowl XXIX, but that wasn't encompass-

ing enough for Devaney.

"This was worse because we got physically whipped this game," Devaney said.

The Chargers gained 33 yards rushing and their offensive line was overrun by the Packers' front four.

On defense, the Chargers mounted ample pressure early, but quarterback Brett Favre danced away from it to hurt them downfield.

Then, when the Chargers resorted to wholesale blitzing in an attempt to keep the score down, the Packers' offensive line blocked them anyway and enabled the running backs to finish with 126 yards in 30 carries.

NFL history tells us that teams that run the ball and stop the run win championships.

After three cakewalks, the Packers have gained 139, 171 and 132 yards on the ground, the first time during Holmgren's tenure and the first time since the mid-1990s that they have rushed for 100 yards or more in three straight games.

Meanwhile, their first three opponents have mustered 59, 59 and 33 yards on the ground.

"We don't want to be known as just a

Jeffrey Phelps

The league's top-ranked defense shows Chargers running back Leonard Russell that he has nowhere to go but down. The Chargers managed just 33 yards on the ground.

LeRoy Butler gets a hand from the fans at Lambeau Field after returning an interception 90 yards for a touchdown.

Dale Guldan

finesse team," Packers defensive tackle Gilbert Brown said. "And we're trying to instill it in the other team."

Despite their astonishing start, the Packers still don't have sole possession of first place in the NFC Central. They can secure that Sunday when the division's two undefeated teams, Green Bay and Minnesota, meet in Minneapolis.

"It's not just another game," defensive end Sean Jones said. "I was thinking about that game in the third quarter today.

The Packers have been slow starters under Holmgren — they are a combined 5-7 in the first three games from 1992-'95. That has changed. Only one team in Packers history (1919) has scored more than the current team's 115 points in the first three games of any season. The point differential of plus-89 (115-26) is the most favorable since the 1962 club outscored its

Chargers quarterback Stan Humphries is helpless to block LeRoy Butler's path to the end zone with a 90-yard interception return.

Rick Wood

first three opponents, 100-7.

The sheer dominance of their September outburst was enough for someone to ask Holmgren about comparisons to Vince Lombardi's dynasty.

"That would be very flattering," Holmgren said. "But I have always said that that group of men and Coach Lombardi and that era will never be duplicated. Now, if we can approach some of that at some point, great."

It didn't take long for the Packers to establish their superiority. The first time Chargers quarterback Stan Humphries took a deep drop, Jones bulled through tackle Harry Swayne for a sack.

After a punt, Edgar Bennett capped a 55-yard touchdown drive with a 10-yard sweep into the end zone.

It wasn't a situation where yards came easily. The Chargers' unorthodox zone coverages behind blitzes led by Junior Seau caused Favre some problems.

Still, Favre made more than enough big plays — Robert Brooks was superb with another 100-yard day — to keep his team in command.

"We were having trouble getting the guy down, so we had to gamble to make him do something in a hurry," Chargers linebackers coach Dale Lindsey said about Favre. "But if you can run the ball the way they can pass the ball, now you're totally off balance."

The Chargers' plan on defense was clear: Double-team White as often as possible. Their problem was that neither Swayne nor his backup, Tony Berti, could handle Jones, and their interior linemen had their hands full with Santana Dotson and Brown.

San Diego settled for 141 total yards, the fewest allowed by the Packers since Detroit had 128 in the 10th game of 1989.

"We were grasping at the end," Ross said. "We just took a good, old-fashioned butt-kicking. It started early, and it didn't really stop."

Green Bay	7	0	14	0	21
Minnesota	7	7	3	13	30

Nobody's Perfect: Vikings Win Big

Robert Smith finished with 88 yards rushing but his 37-yard touchdown run put the Vikings ahead to stay in their 30–21 victory at the Metrodome.

Jeffrey Phelps

MINNEAPOLIS — This was unconditional defeat. Borderline domination. Complete failure.

Maybe the Green Bay Packers still can be the super team that their eager fans and some of their own players expect. But now it's possible their Dec. 22 meeting with the Minnesota Vikings at Lambeau Field could decide the NFC Central title.

"Yes, with the defense they have, the Vikings will be there in the end," Packers safety LeRoy Butler said with a heavy tone of resignation in his voice. "Every year it's the same interview. I just can't believe it."

The Vikings won the hard way Sunday, 30-21, twice rallying behind a furious pass rush that overwhelmed Green Bay's offensive line, turned Brett Favre into a mere mortal and left Coach Mike Holmgren's game plan in ruins.

Some in the Green Bay locker room tried to pass off the defeat, the Packers' first after three lopsided victories, as just another in a string of bizarre occurrences at the Metrodome.

Even Holmgren, who ought to know better, said: "It came down to pretty much the same thing, I think. We made too many turnovers and had too many penalties."

But the turnovers were even at four each, and the eight penalties against the Packers were one more than the Vikings.

No, the improbable plays that have characterized this series evened out. What wasn't even was the pass rush and offensive line play by the teams, which weighed heavily in favor of the Vikings (4-0) and stamped them as a likely force to be reckoned with.

This electrifying matchup was everything but a fluke.

Jeffrey Phelps

Brett Favre is the NFL's top-rated passer but he has no place to hide as the Vikings hand the Packers their first loss of the season.

The Packers are a far different team on turf. This was their fifth consecutive defeat at the Metrodome, and it left Holmgren with one victory in his last 13 games on turf.

The Vikings didn't take the lead for good until four minutes remained, but the crowning blow — Robert Smith's 37-yard touchdown run through the heart of the Green Bay defense — was the product of the Vikings' stubbornly effective strategy. Smith was stuffed all day, but the pinpoint passing of soon-to-be 40-year-old Warren Moon on third down enabled the Vikings to run Smith 26 times until the exhausted Packers finally broke.

"We believed we could run the football, so we had balance in the fourth

A Minnesota fan hangs Brett Favre in effigy during the Packers' fifth straight loss in the Metrodome.

Jeffrey Phelps

quarter," said Vikings Coach Dennis Green, savoring his 7-2 record against Holmgren. "I think that anybody who loves NFL football would have loved this game. It was a great crowd."

But the 64,168 fans weren't the Packers' undoing, because an estimated 15,000-20,000 of them were screaming for Green Bay.

"They said, 'Look, we have a better team,'" Butler said. "'We'll just try to mash it down your throat.'"

Basically, that is what the Vikings did.

Minnesota's seven sacks were the most against Favre, who had not been sacked more than four times since Week 3 of 1994. Not since Week 9 of 1990, when the Raiders had eight sacks, had Green Bay allowed as many as seven.

Meanwhile, Holmgren's attempts to stem the onslaught flopped. Minnesota's linebackers swallowed up the screen game. The Packers' running backs, so potent on grass the last three weeks, gained 35 yards on 13 carries.

Remarkably, not once in 16 possessions did Green Bay sustain a drive. The Packers mustered eight first downs, their low in any game since Week 7 of 1991 against Chicago.

Butler fretted about what the disappointment might do to the club's psyche as the road swing continues in Seattle and Chicago. Others saw it as as an aberration.

"We're still the best team in the league," defensive end Sean Jones said. "I don't care what anyone says. I'm not worried about it."

Packers fans had reason to cheer when Don Beebe ran out of gas after scoring on an 80-yard reception to bring the Packers to within 17-14 in the third quarter.

Antonio Freeman (front) gets a congratulatory hug after making his second touchdown catch of the game.

Tom Lynn

Packers' Express is Back on Track

SEATTLE — Minnesota goes to Giants Stadium and finds a way to lose. The Green Bay Packers go to the Kingdome and take over as if they own the joint.

Super Bowl contenders don't slip up against the weak sisters of the NFL, no matter where the game is played. As much as their loss to the Vikings on Sept. 22 damaged the Packers' collective psyche, their 31-10 victory over the Seattle Seahawks on Sunday should help their confidence.

Green Bay's remarkable coast-to-coast fan base deserved a major assist. Despite the recent widespread apathy toward the Seahawks, the Kingdome remains a harrowing place for visitors, even with 40,000 in the house.

The crowd was 59,973, but with an estimated 15,000-20,000 cheering for the Packers, the hometown fans were never a factor.

Yes, Chris Warren rushed for 103 yards and the Packers' offense endured a 38-play, 130-yard first-half performance. Yet the outcome was never in doubt because the Packers were far superior and, under Coach Mike Holmgren, seldom take anything for granted regardless of the opponent.

"We came in and played decent," Green Bay linebacker George Koonce said. "We didn't play nowhere up to our potential."

Perhaps that was the most impressive angle of the victory, Green Bay's fourth in five games. With the Vikings losing to the Giants,

the teams are tied atop the NFL Central. The Detroit Lions are 3-2.

"Defensively, we wanted to dominate and give Brett good field position," defensive tackle Santana Dotson said, referring to quarterback Brett Favre, who threw four touchdown passes. "I think we did that. I expect to see them (the Vikings) again. Then we'll settle it in Lambeau."

Green Bay had to overcome the loss of wide receiver Robert Brooks, who suffered a concussion on the first play from scrimmage. Still, it seemed just a matter of time before Favre would make some big plays.

In their stadium, the Seahawks are one of the better pass-rushing teams that Green Bay will face. But after a week of soul-searching, the Packers' offensive line held up beautifully, and by early in the third quarter the issue was decided.

"It wasn't our best offensive game," Holmgren said. "But when you win a game when you're not playing well offensively, that's OK. I'll take it any time on the road. This is a difficult place to play."

Reggie White, looking like a running back, rambles 46 yards with an interception in the Packers' 31-10 victory at the Kingdome.

Packers defensive tackle Gilbert Brown sticks his head into the action, bringing down Seattle running back Chris Warren.

Tom Lynn

Packers cornerback Craig Newsome intercepts a Rick Mirer pass at the Kingdome.

Benny Sieu

Green Bay is 4-1 for the first time in a non-strike season since 1978.

"When you're a good team you just have to dominate," safety LeRoy Butler said. "Mike Holmgren doesn't want us just to win. He wants us to dominate. That's a word he's been using since minicamp."

Seattle's only chance was to exercise a ball-control offense behind Warren, a franchise running back. But his first eight carries went for 13 yards as defensive tackle Gilbert Brown overpowered Seattle's guards and center while his teammates gang-tackled with gusto.

That forced the game into the lap of quarterback Rick Mirer, who proved again that he isn't capable of making the throws necessary to bring his excellent supporting cast of wide receivers and tight ends into focus.

What killed Seattle, ultimately, were five turnovers, compared with none for Green Bay. Four of the turnovers led to 24 Packers points.

In 19 games last season, counting the playoffs, the Packers forced 22 turnovers. After five games this season, they have forced the same number.

"Our defense is just a lot faster than it was last year," Packers general manager Ron Wolf said. "Another thing that's really good is we're playing a lot smarter."

Three of Mirer's interceptions — a fourth came on a Hail Mary attempt at the end of the first half — came at the worst times for Seattle: at the end of sustained drives that had the crowd threatening to become a factor.

Favre didn't come close to throwing an interception. That's discipline, which is now such a part of Favre's makeup. It also stems from continuity and experienced leadership throughout the organization.

Those are areas in which Favre and the Packers were light years ahead of the Seahawks.

Green Bay	0	20	14	3	37
Chicago	0	3	3	0	6

A Picture-Perfect Day to Stuff Bears

CHICAGO — In the off-season, the Chicago Bears had plotted revenge for two years of general humiliation at the hands of the much-hated Green Bay Packers, and this picturesque Sunday afternoon at Soldier Field was to be their moment for redemption.

But it was not.

The Bears still ended up being destroyed, 37-6, by a single-minded Packers team that demonstrated not an ounce of pity for their injury-riddled rivals before an early-exiting crowd of 65,480.

Besieged by injuries, Bears coach Dave Wannstedt had used the adversity angle as best as he could, whipping his team into a pregame frenzy.

The heavily favored Packers went three-and-out and punted, then turned it over the next time when the Bears' tactical planning to thwart Favre paid off on a double-teaming deflection of a pass to Robert Brooks and an interception at the Green Bay 45.

Then the Bears drove down the field. On third-and-8 at the 13, Chicago offensive coordinator Ron Turner couldn't have found a better matchup: receiving-type tight end Ryan Wetnight deep in the corner of the end zone against a linebacker.

Receiver Antonio Freeman's lunging catch for a touchdown — despite perfect coverage from the Bears' Kevin Miniefield (24) — was one of several bright moments in a 37-6 victory at Soldier Field.

It was Antonio Freeman's show-case game as the receiver (far left) gathers in a 50-yard 'Hail Mary' pass to end the half.

Bears defenders are in hopeless pursuit of Don Beebe on his third-quarter, 90-yard kickoff return.

But that linebacker was Wayne Simmons, one of many emerging players on the Packers' roster who has made this their best team since the Vince Lombardi era.

Dave Krieg's pass was perfect, Wetnight saw it coming all the way and Simmons was unable to turn back to the ball.

They leaped as one and fell to the grass together, with most of the crowd exploding in exultation. But it wasn't a touchdown; amazingly, it was an interception.

As he ripped the ball from Wetnight's arms, Simmons also ripped the heart out of the Bears.

With eight starters out of the lineup and their leading rusher also injured, the Bears had to perform at fever pitch for 60 minutes with few miscues to overcome their personnel deficiencies.

Simmons, though, struck the first blow to the Bears' confidence, and then a flood of big plays turned the 151st Packers-Bears game into a laugher.

"Domination is when you put a linebacker on a tight end in a situation where 90% of the time he's open, and you get an interception," Packers safety LeRoy Butler said. "... It was the biggest play of the game.

"We hurt them. Don't take anything away from our victory because of their injuries."

Besides the eight starters, the Bears lost cornerback Donnell Woolford (hamstring) and nickel back Kevin Miniefield (concussion). Late in the game, they had

Bears defensive back Marty Carter intercepts a Brett Favre pass, the quarterback's only flaw of the day in a four-touchdown, 246-yard performance.

Jeffrey Phelps

two limping cornerbacks, plus a scrub safety in the lineup.

Against a healthy Green Bay team, the Bears had about as much chance as Forrest Gregg's clubs had against Mike Ditka's powerhouses in the 1980s.

In other words, none.

Nevertheless, Wannstedt must live with his 1-6 record against Mike Holmgren. For the first time since 1960-'62, the Packers have won five straight against the Bears. The 31-point margin of victory matched Green Bay's largest in Chicago.

Still, the Packers remain tied with Minnesota at 5-1 in the NFC Central.

"I have no explanation ... but we have played good football against them," Holmgren said.

Favre had four touchdown passes and a fifth called back before giving way to Jim McMahon for the final series. The Bears limited the Packers' top three running backs to 59 yards on 19 carries.

Packers cornerback Doug Evans' (left) third interception of the season was cause for celebration with LeRoy Butler.

Victory is just a foot away as Chris Jacke kicks a 53-yard, game-winning field goal in overtime of another gem at Lambeau Field.

Benny Sieu

| San Francisco | 0 | 17 | 0 | 3 | 0 | 20 |
| Green Bay | 6 | 0 | 8 | 6 | 3 | 23 |

Jacke Gives 49ers the Boot in OT Win

GREEN BAY — Chris Jacke, sometimes labeled as a selfish player by his colleagues, became a hero of heroes for the Green Bay Packers on Monday night.

Jacke's lackluster start to his eighth season in Green Bay turned to jubilation when he kicked a 53-yard field goal 3:41 into overtime to give the Packers a 23-20 victory over the San Francisco 49ers before a record crowd of 60,716 at Lambeau Field.

"I'd hate to play them again," Packers quarterback Brett Favre said, adding that it was the most physical game he had ever played. "But it may happen. That 2-minute situation ... that's as tough as it gets. Whew. They're a hell of a football team. We just found a way to do it."

It was the fifth field goal of the night for Jacke, who had missed three of his first 10 field goals plus an extra point in the first six games. With his contract set to expire in mid-February, he was not on an impressive roll.

All was forgotten, though, when Jacke ended one of the more memorable games of the Ron Wolf-Mike Holmgren era in Green Bay

The Packers improved to 6-1 — the best record in the NFL — and into first place in the Central Division.

Moreover, it added legitimacy to their Super Bowl hopes and their bid to overhaul the 49ers as one of the two dominant teams in the NFC. Green Bay will have a chance to overtake the other on Nov. 18 against the Cowboys in Dallas.

"It was one of those great games," Holmgren said. "Two real fine football teams going at it tooth and nail.

"We talk about the steps we've taken. Tonight, against this team, coming back, that's something we haven't done quite like this. And it will help us down the road."

San Francisco, a six-point underdog, is 4-2. But this was a much more resilient and stubborn 49ers squad than the one that was crushed by the Packers in the postseason last January.

Without Steve Young, their injured quarterback, the 49ers played a resourceful game behind Elvis Grbac and had the lead until the final eight seconds of regulation, when Jacke's 31-yard field goal forced overtime.

It was Green Bay's 21st victory in its last 22 regular-season and postseason games at Lambeau Field.

Favre, under intense pressure throughout from the 49ers' defense, completed 28 of his club-record 61 attempts for 395 yards.

Reggie White leaves the field after his team's 23–20 overtime victory pushed the Packers' record to 6–1.

Receiver Jerry Rice catches a second-quarter touchdown pass despite coverage by Craig Newsome and Mike Prior (39).

Packers tight end Keith Jackson carries 49ers Tom McDonald (left) and Ken Norton Jr. during a 50-yard pass play in the first quarter.

Don Beebe, subbing for the injured Robert Brooks, had a career game with 11 receptions for 220 yards and one score. Brooks suffered knee ligament damage on the Packers' first play and will need season-ending surgery.

After a sluggish start, dominated by Green Bay's defense, the 49ers struck for 17 points in the final six minutes of the first half to take a 17-6 halftime lead.

San Francisco had poor field position and produced just two first downs on its first five possessions. But the Packers could generate just two field goals despite twice starting first-half drives from the 49ers' 49.

Meanwhile, Grbac had little time to pick out receivers as the Packers' front four pressured hard early with the benefit of crowd noise and field position. Finally, Grbac gained some breathing room on completions of 17 yards to Ted Popson and 24 yards to Jerry Rice midway through the second quarter.

Tommy Vardell provided a threat on the ground and Grbac completed 5 of 5 passes for 30 yards. The Packers hurt themselves when defensive end Sean Jones lost his composure and kicked Popson in the side for a 9-yard penalty for unnecessary roughness.

Green Bay's pass rush lost some steam as well as the half wore on. Grbac had all day to throw on his first scoring pass to Rice.

The 49ers struck again when defensive tackle Dana Stubblefield fell off into coverage and intercepted Favre's short pass to Edgar Bennett.

Offensive coordinator Marc Trestman

Tom Lynn

Brett Favre signals touchdown after receiver Don Beebe scored on a controversial 59-yard touchdown pass. Beebe's knee appeared to be down but the officials ruled there was no contact and the touchdown stood.

Packers receiver Robert Brooks leaves the field for the last time with a season-ending knee injury.

then succeeded in matching Rice against Craig Newsome on second-and-5 at the Green Bay 13. Rice stutter-stepped outside against Newsome and Grbac made a tough throw to the boundary for the touchdown.

The Packers got back into contention midway through the third quarter on a controversial touchdown pass of 59 yards to Beebe. He made the catch on a broken play 29 yards downfield. It appeared as if cornerback Marquez Pope touched Beebe on the ground but the officials ruled otherwise and the touchdown counted.

Then Bennett made a gutsy dive into the end zone on a pass for the 2-point conversion, cutting the 49ers' lead to 17-14.

As the game wore on the Packers' defense took control while their offense was effective enough to drive 50 yards on 15 painstaking plays to set up Jacke's tying 35-yard field goal with 3:35 left.

But Favre's slant pass for rookie Derrick Mayes was intercepted by Pope, setting up a 28-yard field goal by Jeff Wilkins with 1:50 remaining. "I've thrown it a million times," Favre said. "You assume the receiver will beat him but the guy made a great play."

Nevertheless, the 49ers' conservative plan wasn't enough to prevent Favre from completing 4 of 5 passes for 34 yards. That set up Jacke for a 31-yard field goal with eight seconds left that brought overtime.

"I guess they figured with their defense, three points would be enough," Favre said. "I can't say we've played a tougher defense than that.

"In a game like this stats don't matter. It's just a matter of who makes plays."

Photo on Pages 56-57 by Tom Lynn

The going was tough for running backs on both teams, including 49ers running back Tommy Vardell, who struggles for extra yardage against Gilbert Brown.

The Faithful Following Goes Coast-to-Coast

Green Bay — Saturday night in Kansas City: Party hearty, then spill out of a sports bar and almost halt downtown traffic.

Sunday morning in St. Louis: Attend church services at the Old Cathedral near the base of the Arch and hear compliments from the priest on the shade of green in your garb.

Sunday afternoon in Chicago: March gaily back up Michigan Avenue, victory in hand and the Loop at your feet.

Packers fans.

They were everywhere in 1996, determined as never before to support the team from the NFL's smallest city.

Some flew to road games from Wisconsin, jamming commercial flights to the last seat week after week.

But many others, with little or no hope of ever scoring a seat at Lambeau Field itself, spread out across the country to spread the legend of Main Street USA and the club Packers president Bob Harlan labeled as "America's real team" after a spot in the Super Bowl was secure.

The cheese-headed frenzy made for endless fun along the road to New Orleans and countless wisecracks from big-city sophisticates at every stop. Most significantly, it probably helped the Packers finish with a 5-3 record away from Lambeau,

their first winning season on the road in 24 years.

At all eight of the stadiums visited by the Packers, from Tampa to Seattle and six locales basically in between, people in the ticket offices reported that no other team even came close to Green Bay in level of fan support.

"It was far and away the highest number for a visiting team I've ever seen here," Chicago Bears ticket manager George McCaskey said. "But what stuck in my mind was the times I've been to Lambeau Field and knowing Bear fans were so far and few between there."

Using estimates from each ticket

Second-year guard Adam Timmerman is the center of attention as young fans accompany him on his way to Lambeau Field during training camp.

Edgar Bennett scores the first touchdown Sept. 15 against San Diego and is swarmed by jubilant fans after his Lambeau Leap into the seats.

department, an educated guess is that almost 100,000 of the 522,749 fans who saw the Packers play on the road were cheering for them. Combine that 20% with the noise-making intensity of fired-up Packer fans and the home-field advantage often was partially negated.

"They've taken on the aura of a national team now," St. Louis Rams publicist Rick Smith said. "It was the first game where a visiting team's presence, colors and noise was in the dome. You could feel the electricity in the air for the Packers."

Never before had the Packers received anywhere near this level of support on the road. Minnesota, Tampa Bay and Detroit usually had solid pockets of Packer backers, but nobody was prepared for the vast migration to Seattle in late September.

More than 20,000 Green Bay fans, many of whom flew or drove from California and across the Pacific Northwest, gave the Seahawks their only sellout of the season at the Kingdome. Stunned Seahawks officials said none of their opponents in the two decades of their existence ever had more than 1,000 of their fans in attendance.

"It could have been a hornet's nest," Green Bay linebacker George Koonce said. "But we had 35% or 40% of the crowd for us."

Another thorny obstacle was made much easier in Week 15 when about 25,000 Packers fans turned the Pontiac Silverdome into a sea of green and gold.

They came way early and stayed way late, enjoying every last second of their heroes' 31-3 shellacking of the Lions.

"If anything, because of the number of Green Bay fans, you felt so alone out there," Detroit tackle Scott Conover said. "I'll never forget that feeling."

In Green Bay, the madness knew no bounds. For some, you don't go to Lambeau Field anymore just to watch a game. More and more it has become a

What better way for fans to kick off the season than to gather in Tampa and toss around a beer keg while waiting for the game against the Buccaneers?

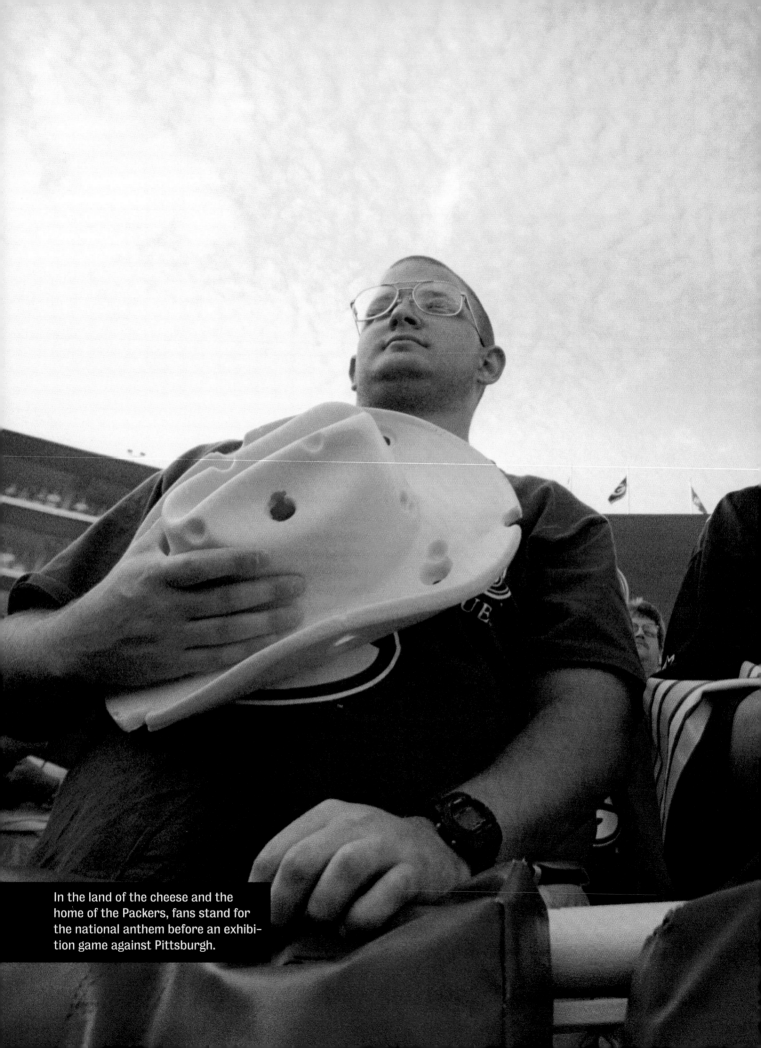

In the land of the cheese and the home of the Packers, fans stand for the national anthem before an exhibition game against Pittsburgh.

Mecca for pro football fans, and the adjective "historic" seems almost fixed in first reference to the 40-year old stadium or "shrine" as many call it.

After walking through one of the 38 entrances, a spectator encounters 60 intimate rows of bench-type seating, three decks of private boxes, the names of the team's Hall of Fame players and championship teams in yellow on the green upper facing, and the overwhelming feeling of football tradition.

The canned music can be a bit annoying but Vince Lombardi wouldn't complain too much. There's still natural grass, and the fans have never stopped taking their football seriously.

"I love it," Packers coach Mike Holmgren said. "For me, it's really a football stadium. Even take the green paint; there is not another stadium like it, looking from the outside. Inside, there isn't a bad seat in the house and the grass is good."

Lambeau has been sold out since 1961 and the waiting list for tickets, which was at 20,007 in August 1995, was more than 28,000 by the end of 1996.

One indication of the phenomenal hold the Packers have in Wisconsin was this season's count of unused tickets. Just 3,909 of a possible 607,900 seats in 10 games weren't filled, with a high no-show count of 1,484 against Minnesota and a reported low of three against San Francisco.

"It's the most appreciative crowd in the NFL," said Dale Lindsey, a San Diego Chargers assistant coach in 1996 who has spent 30 years in the league as a player and coach. "Everybody else through the whole league thinks they're so (expletive) sophisticated and they can't get up and dance and jump around and cheer. These people are a lot more into the game."

Two years ago *The Sporting News* ranked fans in Green Bay as the best in the NFL, and after what transpired this season there would be little reason to suggest a change.

Photo on Pages 62-63 by Jeffrey Phelps

Lambeau groundkeepers take chunks of Lambeau's new sod to go with their memories of the Packers' NFC Championship Game victory over Carolina.

Up to 5,000 spectators, about 20% more than in the last few seasons, stood four or five deep ringing the practice field day after day during training camp.

Refusing to adopt the greed-is-good practices of Cowboys owner Jerry Jones, the Packers had 40,000 nonpaying fans watch their intrasquad scrimmage in July.

Packermania ran rampant in every town and village throughout the state. For six months taverns planned their special-event calendar around the Packers, and the numbers of women and children caught up in the hysteria boggled the mind.

Sales of Packers merchandise and apparel hit record levels, tons of employers allowed their employees to wear green-and-gold to work on

Fridays, and some firms even encouraged impromptu pep rallies in the office before home games.

In 1996, the Packer Hall of Fame came close to doubling its previous attendance record.

"We had some great fans in Buffalo," receiver Don Beebe said, "but the Packers are a way of life here."

Before the divisional playoff game, the Packers put out the word that they needed a temporary work force to help remove snow from the seats at Lambeau Field. So many people showed up that officials had to turn away dozens for the $6-an-hour jobs. Many stayed anyway and worked for free.

Benny Sieu

The glow of the NFC Championship Game victory over Carolina keeps this fan warm long after his fellow fans have departed.

"I said, 'I don't want the money, I just want to help,'" said Rick Fleury, 50, of Green Bay. "I just wanted to be a part of it. It's really thrilling."

Only in Green Bay. Of course.

"I feel I'm involved with the preservation of a national treasure," Harlan said. "We make our money from football and we spend our money for football. That's why we exist."

Harlan is the only chief executive officer in the league whom you can reach by phone without identifying yourself.

Kathy Holmgren, Mike's wife, volunteers at a soup kitchen in Green Bay on Fridays.

When a woman ticketholder in the end zone expressed fears of being squished during the "Lambeau Leap," the security staff put out flyers asking fans in the first six rows not to press forward.

"The Packers tug on the heartstrings of America," said Brian McCarthy, an NFL spokesman involved in marketing.

Benny Sieu

Ten years ago, during the frigid games of December, the overriding color among the fans was blaze orange. Today, it is green and gold.

From 1967, when Lombardi won his last Super Bowl, through January 1992, when general manager Ron Wolf hired Holmgren to replace Lindy Infante, the Packers had four winning seasons and made the playoffs twice. Packers clothing was available in stores, but you had to look

One hopeful fan counts on the lure of a Tickle Me Elmo doll just three days before Christmas to be his ticket into the regular-season finale against Minnesota at Lambeau Field.

hard for it.

This generation of youth in Green Bay was losing the allegiance to the Packers that their fathers and grandfathers had forged during 11 NFL championship seasons.

"(Harlan) ran some survey on the young people here and found out that at some point we weren't going to have anybody in the stands," said Dick Corrick, a personnel executive for the Packers from 1971-'88. "None of the young people could relate to the Glory Years. Then Bob started talking about getting a marketing guy and started promoting."

Besides the losing, the team's image took a beating after a series of off-the-field episodes of sexual misconduct involving Green Bay players.

The fans still snapped up every ticket, but the constant negatives were beginning to take a toll.

Frank Deford of Sports Illustrated came to Green Bay in May 1987 for a nine-page story on the Packers. Entitled "Troubled Times in Titletown," Deford wrote in conclusion:

"Maybe the demographic deck is just too stacked against Green Bay. The scandals and defeats that have brought a sense of gloom and doom to the grand old franchise may seem even worse simply because, deep inside, the good people of Green Bay fear that this may be the way it's going to be from now on."

In 1988, as the Packers were preparing to select Sterling Sharpe with the seventh pick of the draft, Michael Irvin and some of his friends in Miami were shown on TV chanting, "No way, Green Bay; No way, Green Bay."

But then Wolf and Holmgren arrived with their Super Bowl backgrounds, and everything began to change.

The discipline they instilled kept the players off the police blotter. When Reggie White signed as a free agent in April 1993, suddenly it was cool to be both a Packer

Jeffrey Phelps

and a proud Packers fan again.

Leaping into the stands after touchdowns was begun by LeRoy Butler in late 1993, but as recently as November 1994 Wolf would sit in the Lambeau seats gazing upon what he called "this magnificent edifice" and wonder aloud why the fans of Green Bay weren't louder during games.

"It's more like Missouri," Wolf said at the time. "You've got to show me. This place literally sends chills through me. But it's like until you score they don't demonstrate they're with you. You'd like to get that somehow. I don't know how you do it."

As the Packers began to win in Green Bay, however, their captive audience of fans started to become less polite. A new sound system blared forth jock rock. The stadium became fully enclosed with two new Sony Jumbotron scoreboards this season, more effectively keeping sound in.

Harlan's decision in 1995 to play the entire home schedule in Green Bay rather than play three of the eight regular-season games in Milwaukee coincided with the current Lambeau Field winning streak of 18 regular-season and playoff games.

"Lambeau Field now is really, really a great home-field advantage," Holmgren said.

It still isn't as loud as Arrowhead Stadium in Kansas City or one of the domes. But the Green Bay crowds are well past the show-me stage, too.

Packers safety Eugene Robinson, who spent 11 seasons with the Seahawks, has called his first season in Green Bay "just a totally different world."

It is a world in which the social fabric of an entire community, if not a state, is woven around a professional football team.

At least it was in 1996, when the Packers and their fans went to the mountaintop together.

LeRoy Butler sacks Buccaneers quarterback Trent Dilfer, who threw for one touchdown along with two interceptions.

Dale Guldan

Game
8

Tampa Bay	0	0	0	7	7
Green Bay	3	10	0	0	13

Upset in the Making? Just Another Victory

GREEN BAY — Notwithstanding their malfunctioning offense and stumbling special teams, two black-and-white constants in a sea of gray Sunday afternoon made the Green Bay Packers almost immune from shocking defeat.

Truth One: The Packers' defense is bordering on dominant.

Truth Two: The Tampa Bay Buccaneers' offense is without a weapon.

And so the Packers prevailed by the unsightly margin of 13-7 at Lambeau Field against a woeful opponent that was a 17-point underdog.

With the victory, the Packers remained tied with Washington for the top record in the NFC, and their 7-1 start is the best by a Green Bay squad in 30 years.

"We might have lost that game a couple, three years ago," Packers coach Mike Holmgren said. "Fortunately, we were playing at home, and the crowd helped us."

The Packers are 22-1 in their last 23 regular-season and playoff games at Lambeau Field.

But the crowd of 60,627 at times seemed as lethargic as the home team, even at the bitter end in the only moment of high drama.

There was the Buccaneers' defense, high-fiving and hugging off the field after linebacker Derrick Brooks stuffed

Dorsey Levens short of the first down on Holmgren's failed fourth-and-2 gamble at the Tampa Bay 31 with 1:55 remaining.

And there was the Buccaneers' offense, 69 yards from a touchdown that easily would have meant the biggest upset in the league this season.

From the Packers' sound system poured forth over and over a canned invitation to bury the Buccaneers in noise: "We Will, We Will, Rock You!"

Even when Trent Dilfer walked to the line of scrimmage, judging by the moderately raucous response of the crowd, it seemed as though no one took it seriously that the Floridians were any threat to pull it off.

Receiver Antonio Freeman is comforted by teammate Dorsey Levens after Freeman broke his left forearm during a lackluster 13-7 victory over Tampa Bay.

Jim Gehrz

Buccaneers receiver Robb Thomas pays the price after a catch in front of cornerback Doug Evans.

"There really wasn't anything to go to," first-year coach Tony Dungy said.

"They played us man-to-man with tight coverage and a good pass rush. They're the type of defense, it's going to be tough to beat them in that situation."

Dungy, one of the game's finest defensive coaches, offered perhaps the highest praise that Green Bay's No. 1-ranked unit has earned this year.

"They might be the best defense that I've seen in the last six or seven years," Dungy said.

Not that the Buccaneers (1-7) had the wherewithal to offer more than a token challenge.

As presently configured, with Errict Rhett limited to 12 carries after a 93-day holdout and playmakers Jackie Harris and Horace Copeland injured, the impression emanating from the loser's locker room was that 14 first downs and 196 yards of total offense amounted to a decent day's work given the circumstances.

Moreover, if the Buccaneers hadn't botched a punt, blown an attempt for a 27-yard field goal and given the Packers three points by having too many players on the field, their modest offensive production might have been enough.

Because, while Tampa Bay's two longest gains in 58 snaps went for 21 yards, the Packers were almost as punchless with just one gain (a 26-yard pass to Mark Chmura) for more than 18 yards in 70 plays.

"It was kind of a ho-hum day on

Jim Gehrz

All-Pro LeRoy Butler is fired up after making a big play against the Buccaneers.

offense," Brett Favre said. "I expect us to go out and score 30 points."

The day of "near misses," as Holmgren labeled it, started on the first series when Favre underthrew Chmura on a bootleg pass and safety John Lynch intercepted at the Tampa Bay 25.

When the Packers got the ball back, flanker Antonio Freeman had to leave because of a broken bone in his left forearm that will keep him out from 4-6 weeks.

Coupled with the loss of Robert Brooks in the previous game, the linger-

ing ankle injury of Terry Mickens and the refusal of the front office to pay Anthony Morgan more than minimum wage, the Packers had to play 3 $\frac{1}{2}$ quarters with three wideouts: Don Beebe, Desmond Howard and Derrick Mayes.

The results, shall we way, were mixed.

The receivers failed to catch a pass longer than 11 yards, offered almost nothing after the catch, dropped two passes and caught another out of bounds.

Holmgren resorted to new formations (two of four split receivers were tight ends), rare trickery (a flea-flicker, a halfback option pass) and more passing to running backs.

Nothing much seemed to work.

An early push to the Tampa Bay 16 ended with a sack stemming from a blocking mixup. A possible touchdown pass to Keith Jackson was batted down at the line. Favre fumbled an exchange to abort a drive at the Tampa Bay 30.

Howard fumbled a punt return at the Tampa Bay 44. Favre overthrew Howard in the end zone on the 34-yard flea-flicker, then Jacke missed a 46-yard field-goal attempt.

"You play an emotional Monday night game and you have the bye," Holmgren said. "It's a coach's concern.

"We didn't score enough points today, and I thought we were a little careless with the football. But what's our record now? 7-1.

"We won the football game. That's the most important thing."

Detroit	3	7	0	8	18
Green Bay	7	7	14	0	28

New Cast Catches on to 4 Favre TDs

GREEN BAY — It was September 1992 on this very field that Don Majkowski abdicated the throne as the Green Bay Packers' starting quarterback because of an ankle injury against Cincinnati and Brett Favre was crowned king.

If there was even the slightest hint of doubt about the relative merits of the two quarterbacks in the succeeding years, it was erased Sunday.

Favre has been better than he was in a 28-18 victory over the Detroit Lions but never with a more unfamiliar cast of receivers. All he did was throw four touchdown passes as the Packers won for a record 12th consecutive time at Lambeau Field.

"He's clearly the best player in the league," Packers general manager Ron Wolf said about Favre. "What the hell are you going to do?"

The Lions' defense, missing three starters because of injury, nevertheless rang up four sacks with some exceptional individual pass rushes. The last time Favre was sacked as many as four times in a game on grass was in Week 3 of the 1995 season.

Yet, when Favre had to make a play, he did. The Lions would stunt and blitz and disguise coverages and shuffle nickel and dime defenses, but more times than not Favre would escape the pocket or find the open man, sending the frustrated visitors

falling to 4-5.

Green Bay (8-1) has a three-game lead over the collapsing Minnesota Vikings in the NFC Central and owns the best record in the NFC.

"They've got a great team here," said John Teerlinck, the Lions' second-year defensive line coach who held the same job with the Vikings from 1992-'94. "It's the best Green Bay Packer team in my five years in the division.

"You see why he (Favre) was MVP. I thought our pressure was good, but we are young and not fast enough in (the secondary). (Favre) is such a great, great player."

Having won for the 23rd time in their last 24 regular-season and playoff games in Green Bay, the Packers have matched their best start in any season since 1963.

"The players really feel like they can't

Packers safety LeRoy Butler gives Brett Favre a thumbs up sign after Favre passed 65 yards to Don Beebe for a touchdown.

Benny Sieu

Dale Guldan

Don Beebe outruns cornerback Ryan McNeil on his way to scoring on a 65-yard touchdown pass from Brett Favre.

be beat here," Packers coach Mike Holmgren said.

In stark contrast to Favre, 27, was Majkowski, the 32-year-old backup who was pressed into service when Scott Mitchell came up with a rib cartilage injury while throwing in practice Thursday.

Maybe it wasn't the fairest time to evaluate the erstwhile Majik Man, who captivated an entire state in 1989 with his Pro Bowl exploits. He didn't have the benefit of an entire week to prepare.

Defensive end Sean Jones does double duty, slamming former Packers quarterback Don Majkowski to the ground and then going after the loose football.

Benny Sieu

Yet, practice time wouldn't have made much of a difference because Majkowski is what he is: A slightly undersized scrambler with a weak arm and average decision-making skills.

With Mitchell, a strong-armed southpaw who had six touchdown passes in two meetings against the Packers last season, the Lions would have been in an ideal position to win as an 11-point underdog. The reason is that Barry Sanders would gain 152 yards behind an offensive line that didn't back away from challenging Reggie White man-to-man and the rest of the league's top-ranked run defense.

It almost was strictly because of Sanders' phenomenal performance that the Lions became the first team to score

Benny Sieu

Don Beebe is sandwiched by Detroit's Bennie Blades (36) and Ryan McNeil. Beebe and Blades were both shaken up but later returned.

first against the Packers this season and why they trailed, 14-10, late in the third quarter.

But at some point it became clear that Majkowski couldn't keep handing off to Sanders or throwing off run fakes. He had to make plays to beat his old team, and when that time arose, he wasn't up to the task.

The Lions went three-and-out to open the second half.

A moment later, Favre found Mark Chmura on first-and-20 for 14 yards, and passed to Keith Jackson for 17.

Two plays later, Favre ran around after his primary target, Chmura, was covered on a bootleg and eventually found Terry Mickens in the other half of the end zone for a touchdown.

Out came Majkowski again, firing far over the head of his underutilized All-Pro receiver, Herman Moore, and then getting a third-down pass batted back in his face by Santana Dotson.

Two minutes later, Favre laid a perfect 35-yard touch pass on Don Beebe's fingertips for what became a 65-yard touchdown, all but clinching the Packers' fourth division victory in five games.

Detroit settled for 127 net passing yards. Majkowski was sacked five times by a pass rush, led by Dotson, that was frequently intense.

Besides sheer talent, Favre had another tremendous advantage on Majkowski: The Packers are a more disciplined team than the Lions, especially on offense.

Packers linebacker Brian Williams could tell by the looks on the faces of Detroit's three premium wide receivers that they were irritated about not seeing more passes. Moore's body language on some of Majkowski's wounded ducks and his questionable hustle on some routes were evident before the crowd of 60,695.

In what could be the dying weeks of coach Wayne Fontes' regime, there are signs that his players could be ready to jump ship. The Packers under Holmgren are a unified force and have so much ahead of them this season.

At halftime, after Sanders had gained 105 yards, Holmgren erupted when he saw the defensive coaches at the blackboard making adjustments.

"I said, 'No, this is not what's going to do it. It's just playing harder and with more emotion.' In the first half we did not control them defensively," Holmgren said. "In the second half we did."

Gabe Wilkins puts a big hit on Lions quarterback Don Majkowski.

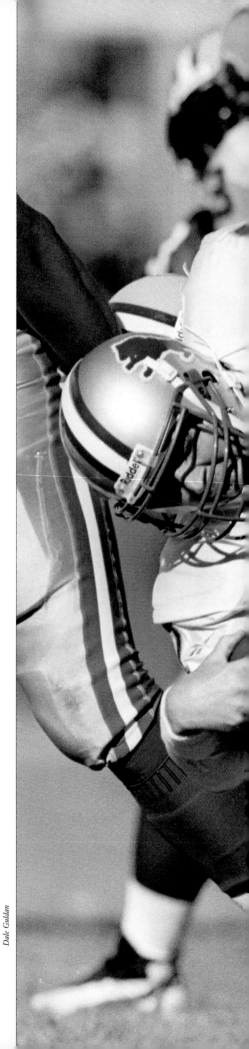

Dale Guldan

Green Bay	3	3	7	7	20
Kansas City	3	17	7	0	27

K.C. Ground Game Grinds No. 1 'D'

KANSAS CITY, MO. — Losing an interconference game by a touchdown in one of the NFL's harshest settings won't stop the Green Bay Packers from reaching the Super Bowl.

Actually, the Packers lost no ground when their closest pursuers in the NFC — San Francisco, Philadelphia and Washington — also lost Sunday.

But if the Packers' 27-20 loss to the Kansas City Chiefs does come back to haunt them, they should remember this afternoon before 79,281 mostly red-clad and rabid fans at Arrowhead Stadium as a game that should have been won.

Packers coach Mike Holmgren actually attempted to pass it off as a nice comeback by a team on the rise after a desultory start, conveniently forgetting that the Packers were a three-point favorite and played in the NFC championship game last season.

"I was proud of my team," Holmgren said. "You can't play a team the caliber of the Chiefs and be that sloppy with the football."

There was no reason in the world for anyone in the Green Bay locker room to be proud.

For the second consecutive week, the Packers' supposedly impregnable run defense was gouged. Last week, it was the greatness of Barry Sanders. This time, the Chiefs rushed for 182 yards behind a corps of five running backs.

Moreover, they really don't have a quarterback, their tackles are below average,

their tight ends are backups and their receivers are a bunch of guys off the street or late-round draft picks.

What the Chiefs do have on offense is a powerful center, Tim Grunhard, and two elite guards, Will Shields and Dave Szott. More importantly, they have a hard-nosed identity developed over time and a realistic approach to their many flaws.

How important was it for the Chiefs to make their running game work?

"We had no chance otherwise," said Jimmy Raye, their running backs coach.

So the Chiefs went stubbornly about their task, rushing 40 times and permitting Steve Bono to pass 23 times. Bono hit some open receivers when play-action passes gave him opportunities, and when the Packers chased him he threw the ball away without incident.

Against the Chiefs' limited arsenal, the Packers' top-ranked defense should have had more than enough personnel to maintain control.

Packers quarterback Brett Favre is drilled into the grass at Arrowhead Stadium in the Packers second loss of the season, 27-20, to the Chiefs.

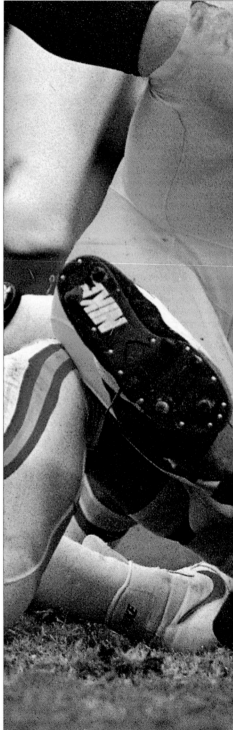

Rick Wood

But Craig Newsome allowed 69 yards on the game-opening play. Marcus Allen, more persistent than explosive at age 36, rushed 10 times for 48 yards. And then his replacement, disappointing former first-round pick Greg Hill, destroyed the Packers for 94 yards on 14 carries and three touchdowns.

"That's the first time this season someone has run on us," Holmgren said. "They got us. It won't happen again."

Green Bay still hasn't had even one of its top 15 or 16 players on defense miss a game because of injury. But the Packers were far from full strength.

Defensive tackle Santana Dotson played with a bad knee. Defensive end Sean Jones left in the first half with a sore ankle. Safety

Jeffrey Phelps

Chiefs fan Monte Short cheers on his team. The Chiefs took the Packers' best shots but managed to win, 27-20.

Eugene Robinson went the distance on an injured ankle. And cornerback Doug Evans, a much better player in run support than rookie Tyrone Williams, was ejected on the first play of the second quarter for bumping an official after a questionable 27-yard penalty for pass interference.

"It was a horrendous call," Packers general manager Ron Wolf said. "There's absolutely no question it should have been interference on the receiver. It took one of our men away from us. That was even worse. It hurt everything we did."

The Chiefs were surprised that the Packers, unlike many of their opponents, played with seven rather than eight defenders near the line of scrimmage. So were some of the Packers.

"The game plan they had was to run the ball," safety LeRoy Butler said. "Be very physical. I think that caught us by surprise."

But it shouldn't have, given the fact that the Chiefs did the exact same thing last week against Minnesota.

With the temperature at 30 and the noise level preventing their tackles from hearing the snap count, this was the time for the Packers to prove that they had the resolve and strength to move the ball on the ground. It was the best chance to slow down the Chiefs' outstanding pass rush, to minimize the crowd noise and to take the game out of the hands of quarterback Brett Favre's suspect wide receivers.

When push came to shove, however, the run wasn't there.

The height of run-game futility came with 6 minutes left when, on fourth-and-2, Edgar Bennett appeared to have the corner on a weak-side sweep but linebacker Anthony Davis stopped him a foot short.

Favre passed for 310 yards and one interception, but he could have thrown three or four by the way he threw the ball .

Don Beebe and Derrick Mayes caught touchdown passes, but it was never more apparent how limited the Packers are without Robert Brooks and Antonio Freeman.

"I can't agree with that," Wolf said. "Who in the hell do the Chiefs got out there? And they're supposed to be a great team.

"I'm not concerned about our weapons or this or that. We've got a very good football team. We like all this praise and all this, but we have to go on the road and win some games."

The Packers' next chance to stop the run and run the ball will be next Monday night at Texas Stadium, where they've done neither against the Cowboys under Holmgren.

Rick Wood

Packers cornerback Doug Evans is flagged for pass interference on a long pass to the Chiefs' Tamarick Vanover and then is ejected for protesting the call and bumping the official.

Another Doomsday in the Heart of Texas

IRVING, TEXAS — The Green Bay Packers were exposed as a wounded, flawed football team before a jeering crowd of 65,032 at Texas Stadium and millions more in their living rooms across the nation Monday night.

The Packers' crusade to defeat the Dallas Cowboys on their home turf after seven consecutive losses instead became an exercise in tedium and futility.

Dallas isn't ready to abdicate the NFC throne, and the Packers aren't ready to take it. That was made abundantly clear in the Cowboys' 21-6 victory over the overmatched Packers, a team that had almost no chance to move the ball with its starting wide receivers and tight end Mark Chmura out because of injuries.

"Excuses are excuses," Packers general manager Ron Wolf said. "I don't think they're appropriate. This is professional football. People have to step up and perform.

"To me, this was an embarrassing game for the Green Bay Packers."

For Cowboys kicker Chris Boniol, it was a record-tying night. Boniol kicked field goals of 45, 37, 42, 45 and 35 yards in the first half and then added two more in the second, tying a NFL record with seven and accounting for all of Dallas' points.

Under siege much of the night, Packers quarterback Brett Favre struggled trying to find open receivers against a Cowboys

defense that featured Pro Bowl cornerbacks Deion Sanders and Kevin Smith and all-pro strong safety Darren Woodson.

"People have to catch the football when it's thrown to them," Wolf said. "That part of the game was very poor tonight.

"I keep hearing we're playing without our receivers. So what? It's part of professional football."

Wolf said he didn't think the loss would be damaging over the long haul, partly because wide receiver Antonio Freeman should return in about two weeks from a broken arm and Chmura has a chance to return in about a month.

"We'll have our team in December, and then we'll see," Wolf said. "Freeman will help us dramatically. But Dallas still is a

Tom Lynn

Michael Irvin leaves Packers cornerback Craig Newsome lying on the turf at Texas Stadium. The Packers found themselves down and out most of the game.

Cowboys wide receiver Michael Irvin grabs for Reggie White during a confrontation late in the fourth quarter of the Packers' seventh consecutive loss to Dallas.

Brett Favre shakes off the effects of yet another pounding administered by the Dallas Cowboys.

dominant team. I saw nothing to think any different."

Favre completed 21 of 37 passes for 194 yards and one touchdown.

It was the third time this season that the Packers lost a road game in a hostile environment. They fell to 8-3, two games ahead of Minnesota in the NFC Central. Washington and Green Bay share the best records in the conference.

"I'm disappointed," Green Bay coach Mike Holmgren said. "It's hard to come down here and not play well. It got a little unruly there at the end, and I don't like to see that.

"They're a good team. You can't make the mistakes we made and get the penalties like we did. The penalties are what bothered me the most."

Dallas improved to 7-4 and assured itself of winning any tiebreaker with the Packers for home-field advantage in the playoffs.

The first half was a case of almost complete Dallas control. The score of 15-0 was made respectable only because the Cowboys played it safe inside the Green Bay 30.

On offense, the Packers seemed out of sorts from the opening series. All five of Green Bay's first-half possessions ended in punts.

The Packers also hurt themselves with careless play. Tackle Earl Dotson was penalized for holding, negating an 18-yard run by Edgar Bennett. Later in the first quarter, a snafu involving substitution of running backs forced the Packers to rush the snap on third-and-2, and Dorsey Levens was stuffed behind the line on a slow-developing play.

Also, the Packers had to blow a timeout on their second series because of an alignment error, and then a third-and-2 pass to Terry Mickens gained 1. That's a cardinal sin rarely committed by Holmgren's teams in the passing game.

Jeffrey Phelps

Jeffrey Phelps

Dallas kicker Chris Boniol celebrates his NFL record-tying seventh field goal of the game in the Cowboys' 21-6 victory.

Dallas outgained the Packers, 213-61, in the first half.

Quarterback Troy Aikman, under little or no pressure, hit an easy 18 of 26 passes for 158 yards in the first half. The Cowboys moved to the Green Bay 27-, 19-, 24-, 26- and 17-yard lines in the first half, but had to settle for field goals each time.

After the teams traded punts to open the second half, the Packers finally mounted a legitimate drive. But the Packers fell short, leaving Chris Jacke to convert a 32-yard field goal. But Jacke's kick sailed left and, with it, the Packers' hopes of a comeback.

Favre managed to put some points on the board late in the game when he connected with Derrick Mayes on a 3-yard touchdown pass on a fade route. The two-point conversion pass was intercepted in the end zone, and another date in Dallas ended on a negative note for the Packers.

Road Swing Ends on a Positive Note

ST. LOUIS — The Green Bay Packers charged from the depths of despair Sunday night to avoid what would have been a colossal and damaging upset loss at the hands of the lowly St. Louis Rams.

Listless and just plain lousy in almost every phase of the game during the first half, the Packers righted themselves after intermission to defeat the Rams, 24-9, before 61,499 at the Trans World Dome.

The victory enabled the Packers to finish a rigorous three-game road swing with one victory against two defeats and lifted their overall record to 9-3, three games ahead of the Minnesota Vikings in the NFC Central.

Moreover, if the Packers defeat Chicago at Lambeau Field on Sunday and the Vikings (6-6) lose at home against Arizona, Green Bay can become the first team to repeat as NFC Central champion since the Bears won five in a row during the 1980s.

Packers coach Mike Holmgren improved his record in domes to 7-9 and his record as a favorite to 40-9. The Packers, a nine-point favorite, found themselves trailing, 9-0, late in the first half before the Rams bungled the return of a punt by Craig Hentrich after a safety.

Fueled by Mike Prior's recovery, the Packers got a 37-yard field goal from Chris Jacke as time expired and then scored 21 unanswered points in the second half to secure the victory.

At 9-3, the Packers and San Francisco 49ers remained tied with the best records in the NFC. But Green Bay maintained the lead for home-field advantage throughout the playoffs because of its overtime victory over the 49ers last month.

As poorly as the Packers played in the first half, they were just as effective in the second half. Their reversal of fortune helped take the noisy throng out of the game and paved the way for the comeback victory.

An interception by Doug Evans that he returned 32 yards for a touchdown on the second play of the third quarter gave the Packers their first lead, 10-9.

It became a lead they would never relinquish.

In fact, the Packers kept getting stronger as the game progressed and were a dominant force at the final gun.

A fumble by Tony Banks on an exchange

A tough day for rookie Rams quarterback Tony Banks: he's sacked three times and fumbles twice during the Packers 24-9 win at the Trans World Dome.

Tom Lynn

86

Rick Wood

Keith Jackson's 6-yard touchdown reception put the Packers ahead, 17-9.

Holmgren came out throwing, with Favre passing on eight of the first 10 snaps on the scripted playlist. The Packers failed to cross the 50 until the final two minutes of the half.

Favre completed 10 of 16 passes for 55 yards. Newly acquired wide receiver Andre Rison played extensively and had three catches for 24 yards.

"Favre looked like he's pressing a little bit," McCartney said. "They didn't throw the ball downfield at all. They're not playing with the confidence they had."

On offense, the Rams stuck to a conservative formula designed to protect Banks, their strong-armed, mobile but inexperienced quarterback. They ran the ball 19 times in the first half compared to 15 passes, totaled a modest 146 yards and posted almost a six-minute edge in time of possession.

Harold Green, starting because rookie Lawrence Phillips was nursing a bruised knee, rushed 12 times for 43 yards. Phillips replaced him midway through the second quarter and had 23 yards on six carries.

For the first time this season, the Packers had a starter on defense missing because of injury. Gabe Wilkins started for Sean Jones, who sat out because of an ankle injury.

from center was recovered by linebacker Brian Williams at the St. Louis 20 midway through the third quarter. That play led to a 6-yard touchdown pass to Keith Jackson.

Then, early in the fourth quarter, the Packers drove 38 yards for another touchdown after a nifty 39-yard punt return by Desmond Howard. It came after a magnificent madcap scramble by Brett Favre, who eluded two sacks in the backfield before spotting Dorsey Levens for a 5-yard touchdown pass.

In the first half, the Packers were pathetic on offense, punting on their first five possessions and absorbing a safety. Only the Rams' failure to field the punt after the safety enabled the Packers to get on the board and trail, 9-3.

Green Bay could muster just two first

downs and 48 total yards against a St. Louis defense that ranked 28th entering the game.

"Obviously, they struggled," said Mike McCartney, a pro scout for the Chicago Bears. "They didn't run the ball at all, but that's never been their M.O. anyway."

The Packers benched Gilbert Brown early in the first quarter and used Darius Holland and Bob Kuberski at nose tackle. Rookie Keith McKenzie took some snaps for Wilkins on passing downs, and even Shannon Clavelle made a one-snap appearance in the second quarter.

The Rams' touchdown came late in the second quarter and capped a 69-yard drive in 13 plays. It came on a third-down pass of 6 yards from Banks to Isaac Bruce in the back of the end zone with safety Eugene Robinson in tight coverage.

"Bruce is a great player," McCartney said. "It was defensed almost perfectly. It took a great throw and catch."

Rick Wood

Brett Favre welcomes new teammate Andre Rison into the fold after Rison's third catch of the day set up a Green Bay touchdown.

Andre Rison is all smiles after helping the Packers get back on track.

Kick return star Desmond Howard (left) and Eugene Robinson celebrate Howard's 75-yard punt return for a touchdown in the Packers' sixth straight victory over the Bears.

Gary Porter

Bears No Match for Holmgren Hex

GREEN BAY — Start over. Hire someone with a fresh idea. Junk what you got here.

Whatever Chicago Bears coach Dave Wannstedt holds near and dear as his defensive philosophy, and he learned much of it from his mentor, Jimmy Johnson, it should be placed in mothballs the next time he coaches against Mike Holmgren.

Another chapter in Holmgren's mastery of Wannstedt was written on a gray Sunday at Lambeau Field as the Green Bay Packers (10-3) frustrated the Bears one more time, 28-17.

The victory was the Packers' sixth in a row over the Bears, the first time that has happened in the ancient rivalry since the Packers won seven straight from 1928-'30. Holmgren is 7-1 against Wannstedt and, once again, it was the offense coordinated by Holmgren that carried the day against the defense coordinated by Wannstedt.

"I can't put my finger on it," Packers quarterback Brett Favre said. "I think Wannstedt is a great coach. I think injuries have had a big part in it. It's kind of weird right now."

Granted, the Bears were without injured linebacker Bryan Cox, "kind of the soul of that defense," according to Holmgren.

But the Bears (5-8) had Cox eight weeks ago and still were destroyed by the Packers, 37-6.

For five consecutive games the Bears hadn't allowed more than 17 points. Then their offense, so limited with Dave Krieg having to play quarterback rather than Erik Kramer, succeeded in hogging the ball for 21 of the first 28 minutes with an impressive short-pass, inside-run formula.

They led, 7-0, and, in the words of Tony Wise, their assistant head coach/ offensive line coach, "We had them reeling a little bit."

Only 1:24 remained in the first half, and the crowd of 59,682 was on edge. Not only were the Bears controlling both lines of scrimmage, but Wannstedt was operating in devil-may-care fashion, twice disdaining field goals to go for it on fourth down and even lining up wide receiver Curtis Conway for one play at quarterback.

Even as a 10-point underdog against an adversary that had won 23 of its previous 24 regular-season and playoff games at home, the Bears could look toward the second half with confidence.

Holmgren and his on-field conductor, Favre, saw 84 seconds to tie. And in four plays they did, shredding the Bears' secondary for 60 yards on three rapid-fire completions.

For 29 minutes, the emotionally charged Bears had kept Favre under wraps and halted the Packers' running game dead in its tracks. In fact, Holmgren didn't even try to run, passing 12 times compared with six rushes for 13 yards.

Holmgren came out firing some more, passing five times in a row to open the third quarter. But then, using his array of personnel groupings and motion to keep the Bears off balance, he returned to a staple of previous victories over Chicago — draw plays against nickel defenses — to spring Dorsey Levens for gains of 16 and 15 yards.

When the fourth quarter began, the conventional ground game finally was there for Green Bay as Levens hammered 24 yards behind William Henderson's lead block out of an I-formation to the Bears' 17.

On the next play, with the Packers clinging to a 14-10 thanks to Desmond Howard's 75-yard punt return, Wannstedt retaliated by running up safeties Marty Carter and Anthony Marshall on either side of center Frank Winters in an obvious blitz look.

The problem was that there still were 12 seconds left on the play clock. Favre, displaying the poise instilled in him by Holmgren, calmly stood up, called an audible and then flicked a 7-yard slant pass to Don Beebe when the Bears went ahead and blitzed anyway.

On the next play, Wannstedt went

Tom Lynn

Raymont Harris discovers why the Packers have the top-ranked defense in the NFL.

Receiver Antonio Freeman is drilled into the turf by Chicago's Walt Harris.

back to another all-out, seven-man pass rush, but the call from Holmgren was an off-tackle run. The Bears were out-flanked, leaving Levens an easy 10-yard gap for a touchdown and an insurmountable 21-10 lead.

"They're dogging, and Dorsey takes it in for a touchdown. ... Unbelievable game he played there with their defense," Packers general manager Ron Wolf said about Holmgren. "The great thing about him is his ability to play chess. Plus, he's got the thing that those really good gamblers have. Like Maverick on TV ... at the right moment."

The Packers ended up rushing 14 times for 76 yards in the fourth quarter and finished with 126 total rushing yards.

Wannstedt seemed to be missing the point when he said, "We weren't con-cerned about (the late first-half touch-down) beating us. If they had driven the ball up and down the field on us, then there would have been concern."

Holmgren's offense is built around big plays, not grinding meat. Any defense that doesn't realize that fact, barring an enormous manpower advantage, is doomed to failure.

"Very rarely today did we get caught by surprise by their blitzes," Favre said. "We were ready for it. We just never had the ball early."

With Antonio Freeman catching five of his 10 passes against rookie cornerback Walt Harris for 75 yards, the Packers gained a modest 342 yards. But their average per play of 6.2 yards was their best since the season opener.

"It's like the wheels came off at our place when we lost two games in a row," Wolf said. "It's due to the fact that we did-n't have our players. You can see now what we have when you put in Freeman and (Andre) Rison and Beebe and (Keith) Jackson. I think we're definitely back to where we were.

"And, there's another piece of the puz-zle here. (Howard) is a devastating return man. Devastating."

"We're all a little (expletive) that we can't take the thing another step," Wise said. "We had them reeling, and then their ability takes over and they rise to the occasion. We should have, too. That's the disappointing thing."

Until Wannstedt does something radi-cally different on defense, it's likely Holmgren and Favre will keep on beating him.

Jeffrey Phelps

Packers offensive lineman Earl Dotson has a head of steam while taking a breather at Lambeau Field.

Packers receiver Antonio Freeman spikes the ball after scoring the first of his three touchdowns in a 41-6 victory over Denver.

Denver	3	0	3	0	6
Green Bay	3	10	7	21	41

Packers' Punch Levels Broncos

GREEN BAY — Brett Favre's brilliant quarterbacking. A mature, opportunistic defense.

More than any other elements, those are the salient reasons why the Green Bay Packers have planted the seed of a dynasty in the NFC Central.

It was fitting, then, that two plays made by Favre and the defense turned a close game against the unmotivated and injury-riddled Denver Broncos into a 41-6 victory before 60,712 Sunday at Lambeau Field.

Everyone had a different spin for a game that meant nothing for the Broncos, who were without their leader, quarterback John Elway, their best offensive lineman, left tackle Gary Zimmerman, and any incentive because they already had wrapped up home-field advantage throughout the playoffs.

"It says we didn't give a damn about this game," Broncos defensive tackle Michael Dean Perry said. "Do you see any real down faces in that locker room?"

However you want to slice it, though, the team with the best record by two games in the NFL had come to Green Bay and suffered its worst loss since November 1988.

"We needed this game a lot more than they did, that's obvious, and John Elway

did not play," Packers coach Mike Holmgren said. "But all those things will not detract at all from what we accomplished today.

"Football players are football players, and coaches are coaches. When you step on the field, don't tell me anyone goes out there not wanting to win. That never happens."

The victory, the Packers' 25th in 26 regular-season and playoff appearances at Lambeau since September 1993, made them the first team since the Chicago Bears of 1984-'88 to win consecutive championships in the NFC Central.

Still, despite a conference-best record of 11-3, the Packers haven't locked up even one home game for the playoffs.

"That is our next step," Favre said. "I think we have a great team, but it's not easy for anyone to go on the road and make it to the Big Show."

Despite their wounds, the Broncos (12-2) scoffed at the possibility of emotional residue should the teams meet again seven

Denver quarterback Bill Musgrave — subbing for starter John Elway — fumbles the ball as he is hit by cornerback Doug Evans. Reggie White recovered the ball and the Packers eventually scored.

Tom Lynn

Jeffrey Phelps

You've heard of turf toe? Strong safety LeRoy Butler comes up with a case of turf face after sacking Bill Musgrave.

weeks from now in the Super Bowl.

"No, not at all," Denver linebacker Bill Romanowski said. "We didn't lose to a superior team. They just outperformed us today. That happens."

"Now, don't be crazy," defensive tackle Jumpy Geathers said. "If we had had No. 7 (Elway), maybe. But it ain't like they came out and boom, boom, boom, boom, right down the field. You saw the first half. Did you see them throwing us around?

"But you take your whipping. If we were going full-go, I could evaluate it better."

Packers general manager Ron Wolf didn't really disagree.

"This got out of hand, but this was in doubt for a long time," Wolf said. "We are what we are, an upper-echelon team in the NFC. The barometer for us has to be Dallas. Until we get over that hurdle ... and it's a significant hurdle, like the Himalaya Mountains."

With 29-year-old dink-baller Bill Musgrave making his first NFL start, the Broncos had no hope to throw downfield and no chance to win unless their defense could hold the Packers to 14 points or fewer.

Musgrave was exposed by the Packers' blitzing defense as the third-stringer that he is. The Broncos finished with 83 yards passing, the lowest total against Green Bay since Detroit mustered 54 in Week 10 of 1989.

Still, the game broke just the way the Broncos wanted.

In the first half, the Packers had four penalties on offense and another one declined. Favre fumbled a center exchange and threw a terrible interception. Antonio Freeman dropped a 13-yard pass. The run blocking at the point of attack was atrocious, leaving Edgar Bennett with 2 yards

Reggie White runs over Broncos tight end Shannon Sharpe to recover a fumble.

on six carries. Mark Chmura slipped and fell when he was wide open inside the Denver 30.

The Packers were clinging to a 6-3 lead with 23 seconds left in the first half when Favre, with a first down at the Denver 14, swung the game inexorably toward the Packers with one of those astonishing plays that only he can make.

Just before the snap, Perry shifted from the tackle-guard gap to a cocked position on center Frank Winters' right shoulder. Perry then exploded past Winters and was clawing at Favre, who increased the speed of his backpedal.

As Perry surged forward, Favre fought him off with a stiff-arm, and Perry collapsed in a heap. Calmly collecting himself

at the 26, Favre scanned the field for a split second and saw Freeman breaking free in the back of the end zone.

With intimidating, 6-foot-7 Geathers charging straight up the middle at him, Favre unleashed a bullet pass that cut between two defenders and was caught by Freeman for a 14-yard touchdown.

"Michael Dean was right on top of him," Denver coach Mike Shanahan said. "Brett gave him a forearm and threw an excellent strike."

The Packers had a 10-point lead, but on the third play of the second half Favre forced another bad interception, which safety Tyrone Braxton returned 14 yards to the Green Bay 28.

Two plays later, it was third-and-3.

If Elway had been in the lineup, odds are the Broncos would have thrown on third down. With Musgrave, Shanahan went with Terrell Davis, but there was no gain.

Jason Elam kicked a 39-yard field goal, but the Broncos had to have a touchdown.

Midway through the third quarter the Packers were flexing their recaptured offensive might that led to a four-touchdown onslaught. Most noteworthy was Freeman, with nine catches for 175 yards and three touchdowns. But the 14-carry, 86-yard rushing performance of Dorsey Levens might have signaled a changing of the guard at running back.

"You've got to give the coaches a lot of credit for getting him the ball," Wolf said.

Packers running back Edgar Bennett's heads-up running has been a strength of the Packers all season.

Green Bay	3	7	6	15	31
Detroit	0	0	3	0	3

Packers at Home in the Silverdome

PONTIAC, MICH. — Never before has a Mike Holmgren-coached team in Green Bay been assessed more than the 11 penalties it earned Sunday.

Nonetheless, the vast differences in discipline and motivation between the Packers in their fifth season under Holmgren and the Detroit Lions in their eighth full season under Wayne Fontes were at the core of the Packers' resounding 31-3 victory before 73,214 at the Silverdome.

Despite their transgressions and first-half sluggishness on offense, the Packers still led, 10-0, at halftime because Holmgren's teams almost never give up the horrendous turnover on offense and are so unified on defense that big plays by opponents have been almost eradicated over the last month.

That's why the Packers are 12-3, why they're on the brink of securing home-field advantage throughout the playoffs and why they've become so hard to beat.

On the other hand, the Lions are 5-10 largely because Fontes is an overly permissive coach whose regime has been marked by dissension, turmoil and finger-pointing, even in good times.

"I think we've kind of fallen apart as a team," Lions quarterback Scott Mitchell said, a stark assessment of an organization in need of a face lift.

And so, with the Silverdome almost vacant of Detroit fans at the end, the Packers walked out in triumph to the shrieks of thousands of green-and-gold-clad fans with their largest margin of victory in a dome since they won at New Orleans, 35-7, in Week 15 of 1981.

"It's so correct; we don't screw up," Packers general manager Ron Wolf said. "Part of our discipline is what our coaches have done. We've got so many things that we can do here to enable us to win a game and stay in a game."

With Brett Favre marshaling a three-touchdown, 231-yard onslaught in the second half, with the defense holding Barry Sanders to a 3.7-yard rushing average and demonstrating superb work against an explosive passing game, and with Desmond Howard dominating the game as few punt returners ever have, the Packers finished the road portion of their season at 5-3.

For the first time since the 1972 team was 6-1 on the road, Green Bay has posted a winning record away from home. And the Packers clinched a first-round bye.

"That's the last thing, one of the harder things that gets done when you're try-

Antonio Freeman's demonstrates his acrobatic skills after a fourth quarter touchdown reception in the Packers' 31-3 victory.

Reggie White puts a big hit on Lions quarterback Scott Mitchell, who folded under the Packers' relentless defensive pressure.

ing to build your program up," Holmgren said of playing on the road. "It's a learned response. It says we're maturing."

Hammering the Lions — who were missing three starters on defense (defensive end Tracy Scroggins, middle linebacker Stephen Boyd and cornerback Corey Raymond) and received only about half a game from nose tackle Henry Thomas and safety Bennie Blades — still represented a major accomplishment.

No matter what, the Lions had the weapons in Sanders' flying feet, Mitchell's big arm, Herman Moore's power and Brett Perriman's quickness to upset the Packers.

What the Lions couldn't afford was the string of boneheaded mistakes that ultimately sucked away the measure of enthusiasm that they brought into the game.

But there was rookie defensive end Kerwin Waldroup losing his cool and hitting Favre a second or two after Thomas fought through his painful groin injury to sack Favre. Instead of forcing the Packers to punt, the Lions had given them a first down with a personal-foul penalty and, six plays later, first blood on a field goal by Chris Jacke.

There was much more futility from the Lions.

Mitchell and Perriman combined for a 5-yard completion on third down when 6 yards were needed. Safety Van Malone turned down a free shot in the middle of the field after Mark Chmura caught a pass for 20 yards. Someone sent out the punting team on fourth-and-3, then Fontes had to call a timeout when he decided to go for it.

At least for public consumption, the

Desmond Howard leaves Lions punter Mark Royals in his wake on his way to a 92-yard punt return for a touchdown at the Silverdome.

Tom Lynn

105

Green Bay players refused to kick the Lions when they were down, but they all knew the score.

"The Lions aren't my concern," wide receiver Antonio Freeman said. "I notice a difference in discipline with our team. And it starts with the coaches."

The Packers were far from paragons of perfection, at least early. Aaron Taylor's holding penalty wiped out Edgar Bennett's 12-yard touchdown on a throw-back screen pass, Favre compounded a bad read with a bad throw for an end-zone interception and Don Beebe's inexplicable decision not to get out of bounds prevented a 30-yard field goal by Jacke at the end of the first half.

"We had six penalties in a row at one point," Holmgren said. "I just refuse to accept that type of play."

So the Packers responded with championship-level play in the second half.

The Lions' game plan was to run Sanders and then run him some more. But with Packers defensive coordinator Fritz Shurmur's players adhering to a disciplined, containment-oriented scheme, Sanders' long run was merely 12 yards in 21 carries.

"To be able to corral that guy is an enormous feat," Wolf said.

"It's just amazing how well we're playing on defense this year," defensive assistant Johnny Holland said.

"It's come with the total package that we have."

LEFT: Eugene Robinson and the Packers defense corral the NFL's leading rusher, Barry Sanders, who managed just 78 yards in the game.

RIGHT: Packers wide receiver Antonio Freeman isn't allowed to jump into the stands anymore, but still finds ways to interact with the fans.

Dale Guldan

Proudly Perched at the Top of NFC

Green Bay — The Green Bay Packers sit on top of the pro football world, and it will take a supreme effort for another team to knock them off it.

Their 38-10 humiliation of the Minnesota Vikings on Sunday at Lambeau Field is what happens when one team reaches astonishingly high levels in execution and intensity in not one, not two but all three phases of the game.

This was a masterpiece to cap the Packers' 13-3 regular season, a performance so special that it removed any shadow of a doubt and stamped them as the clear-cut favorite to win Super Bowl XXXI.

"It's really a thrill to be a part of this," Packers general manager Ron Wolf said. "We're a pretty good football team. But this is just the beginning step."

Yes, the victory was meaningful because

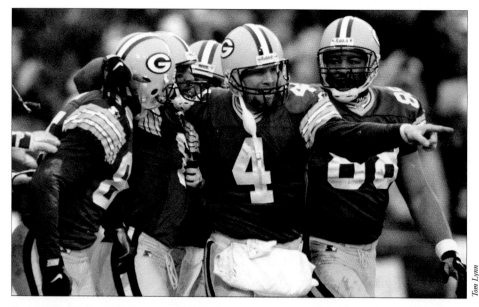

Quarterback Brett Favre celebrates Andre Rison's first touchdown as a Packer with Antonio Freeman (left), Rison, and Keith Jackson (right).

Tom Lynn

Tom Lynn

The running game finally clicked as Edgar Bennett had his first 100-yard game of the season — 109 yards on 18 carries.

Vikings quarterback
Brad Johnson is sacked
by Santana Dotson.

Tom Lynn

it wrapped up home-field advantage for the Packers throughout the NFC playoffs.

The Packers posted the best record of any team in the NFC Central since the Chicago Bears went 15-1 in 1985 and 14-2 in 1986. Green Bay's winning percentage of .813 is the best for the franchise since the 1966 team went 12-2 for an .857 percentage.

For just the third time in 64 years, the Packers finished unbeaten at home (8-0).

And the Packers became the first team to lead the league in points scored (a club-record 456) and fewest points allowed (210) since the Miami Dolphins of 1972.

"You are talking about a lot of great football teams between now and then," Packers coach Mike Holmgren said. "Our players wanted this game badly."

Sure, the statistical milestones were nice, but the Packers had far greater motivation on a 31-degree afternoon. To put it simply, the Vikings had challenged their manhood and the Packers were almost foaming at the mouth ready to respond.

There was the 30-21 loss 13 weeks earlier at the Metrodome in which the offensive line had been embarrassed to the tune of seven sacks.

There were the comments made by linebacker Jeff Brady last week about his plans to go "head hunting" at Lambeau Field.

And early in this game, there was cornerback Corey Fuller gouging Frank Winters in the eyes and then there was Fuller prancing directly in front of the Packers' bench after his wicked, blindsided, fumble-causing hit against Antonio Freeman.

By NFL standards, the Packers as a team usually are a model of restraint. But given all of the above, not to mention the fact that the Vikings were inspired and playing well themselves in a 10-10 first half, the Packers were incited and attacked with a vengeance seldom seen from one of Holmgren's squads.

"That's the first time I ever heard Brett Favre talking trash," said Brady, a Packer

Packers running back Dorsey Levens leaps for some of his 73 yards on 11 carries in the 38–10 victory over the Vikings.

Benny Sieu

from March 1992 until August 1993. "He was talking to our (defensive backs). It was funny. I guess that's how much he wanted it."

At times, the Packers crossed the line. Craig Newsome was way late pushing Cris Carter out of bounds on a sideline route. There were other late hits, by the Vikings as well as the Packers.

All the ill will and bad blood is precisely why the Packers were so exultant in victory. They had weathered the best Minnesota could offer, then blown the Vikings away with the style of play that hurts the most: running it down your throat.

"They challenged physically," Wolf said. "But there's a difference between challenging physically and with the mouth. They challenged with the mouth and got beat."

It has been years since not one but two Packers running backs ran with the resolve displayed by Edgar Bennett and Dorsey Levens. Together, with their punishing lead blocker, William Henderson, and a spirited line that dominated, the Packers rushed for 233 yards, their second-highest total in any game since 1985.

Foge Fazio, the Vikings' 57-year-old defensive coordinator who began coaching in 1961, said the second half, in which Green Bay had four touchdowns, 285 total yards and 19 first downs, was the poorest with which he had ever been associated.

Minnesota coach Dennis Green kept coming back to the fact that the Vikings are built to play on turf, somewhat excusing the performance because of the mushy, newly sodded field.

Fazio was having none of that.

"Just (expletive) terrible," Fazio said. "Got our (expletive) kicked. Just flat (expletive) awful. No excuses. They had to play on the same (expletive) field. They tackled our guys. We couldn't tackle (expletive)."

For the fifth consecutive week, the Packers made the right adjustments after a shaky first half and then routed an opponent in the second half. In those games, they had

Tight end Keith Jackson goes for a slam dunk after scoring a second-half touchdown.

Desmond Howard can't avoid the touchdown-saving tackle of Minnesota punter Mitch Berger after a 47-yard return in the fourth quarter.

Benny Sieu

a point margin of just 43-29 in the first half and then 119-16 in the second half.

On defense, the Packers gave up two first downs after halftime, eliminating the running game, besieging quarterback Brad Johnson and taking away his wide receivers snap after snap with tight, clawing coverage.

"One touchdown in 12 quarters," Packers defensive coordinator Fritz Shurmur said. "It's a hell of a bunch of guys."

On offense, the Packers ran over the Vikings' undersized front seven with power blocking and power running. Favre seemed to be caught up in the go-for-the-jugular

mentality as well, throwing long perhaps more than he has all season.

Finally, on special teams, Desmond Howard set up three of the four second-half touchdowns with returns of 40, 25 and 47 yards while the cover units gave up a long of merely 26 yards on nine kicks.

The Playoffs

A Mud-and-Guts Victory at Lambeau

GREEN BAY — When push came to shove Saturday, the Green Bay Packers shoved, maybe like they have never shoved before in five seasons under coach Mike Holmgren.

Having blown two-thirds of a 21-0 lead over the San Francisco 49ers thanks to two blunders on special teams, the Packers were setting themselves up for what might have been the most catastrophic defeat in club history.

Instead, they immediately seized this NFC divisional playoff game by the throat with a display of rushing power that had never been there for the Packers in seven playoff games under Holmgren.

Their 12-play, 72-yard drive, culminated by Antonio Freeman's recovery of a goal-line fumble by Edgar Bennett for a touchdown, restored order to a disorderly game on a mud-slickened field and effectively eliminated any chance that the 49ers had for the upset.

In what probably was the most momentous game played at Lambeau Field since the Ice Bowl between Green Bay and Dallas in 1967, the Packers throttled the 49ers in the second half and won going away, 35-14.

"There are so many things we can do to attack you," Green Bay general manager Ron Wolf said. "Plus, our guys believe. Not only do they believe, but they go out and play.

"We said all along: You let us play up here in December and January, our guys can run in this stuff. It was proven again today. We're built exactly for this."

Holmgren, savoring his team's 27th victory in 28 regular-season and playoff games in Green Bay, went so far as to agree with some of his players who have said the Packers feel invincible before their crowd in one of the league's most historic venues.

"We're playing well in every facet of the game," Green Bay defensive end Reggie White said. "I think if we do that for two more games we can celebrate the rest of our lives."

The 49ers, who finished their season at 13-5, had to play without quarterback Steve Young (ribs) after the first two series and All-Pro defensive tackle Bryant Young (neck) for the final three quarters.

As an underdog trying to cope with the almost completely healthy Packers,

Desmond Howard evades 49ers Gary Plummer (50) during a 71-yard punt return for a touchdown. Howard returned another punt 46 yards.

Tom Lynn

Photo on Pages 118-119 by Benny Sieu

Starting quarterback Steve Young (right) lasted two series playing with broken ribs before he was replaced by back-up Elvis Grbac.

those were serious losses.

Nonetheless, it was stunning that a franchise with such a winning tradition, pride in performance and a roster of solid, seasoned players was able to offer so little resistance against a team that it had plotted revenge on for 12 months.

"There was a lot of question where the Green Bay Packers belong in the hierarchy in the National Football Conference," Wolf said. "Certainly I think those questions were answered today."

The flying feet of Desmond Howard staked the Packers to a 14-0 lead with the game just nine minutes old. Seven 49ers had a clear shot to tackle Howard on Tommy Thompson's first punt, but he made them all miss for a 71-yard touchdown return.

It was Howard's fifth punt-return for a score this year — one in the exhibition season, three in the regular season, one in the postseason — and rekindled Wolf's disgust that Howard was not selected ahead of Carolina's Michael Bates as the NFC kick returner in the Pro Bowl.

The turf was flying as Dorsey Levens runs through the mud and a 49ers tackler in the Packers' victory.

Jeffrey Phelps

LEFT: 49ers guard Ray Brown and tackle Steve Wallace are covered with mud near the end of the game. The field later had to be resodded for the NFC Championship game.

ABOVE: As time ticks away, 49ers tackle Steve Wallace stands on the sideline, his helmet evidence of a fierce battle fought but not won.

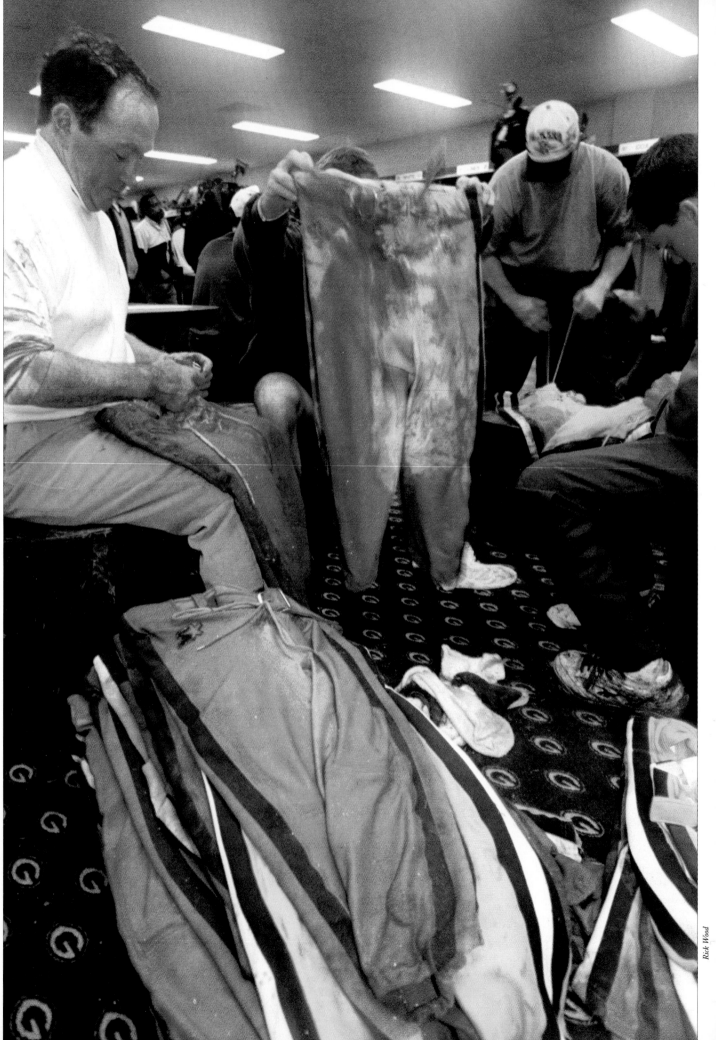

The 49ers spent much of the first half in disarray even though their offensive line, which had been overrun by the Packers in the two previous games, held up amazingly well.

A total of five dropped passes, penalties and blown timeouts added up to enormous negatives for an offense sadly lacking in firepower against a mighty Packer defense.

Still, the 49ers were good enough to convert two breaks for touchdowns. The first came late in the first half after a bouncing punt struck Green Bay defender Chris Hayes in the back of the leg and the 49ers recovered at the Packers' 26.

The second came when Don Beebe muffed the second-half kickoff and the 49ers recovered at the Green Bay 4.

"Shoot, we're in pretty good shape at 21-nothing, then it's a brand-new game," Holmgren said. "At that position, it's easy to kind of get down a little bit. But they didn't."

What happened on the Packers' first possession after the gaffes by Hayes and Beebe was a head coach forgetting the fancy stuff, an offensive line starting to come of age, running backs that refused to go down easily and a San Francisco defense that sorely missed its pre-eminent member.

Not once in the next 12 plays did Holmgren send out his three- or four-receiver formations. Instead, he ran 10 plays with base personnel (six in the I, four in split backs) and two with one back and two tight ends.

He called three passes, but one turned into a 7-yard scramble by Brett Favre. And he called nine runs, with most of them involving straight-ahead zone

Jim Gehrz

Despite rain and the bone-chilling cold, there were only a few no-shows for the Packers-49ers playoff game.

blocking and fullback William Henderson leading through the hole.

After the fourth first down of the drive, the Packers lost 3 yards to the 49ers' 10 on a bad first-down handoff between Favre and Bennett.

But — wonder of wonders — Holmgren went right back to smash-

Jim Gehrz

In some parts of the field, players were deep in mud.

mouth football on second-and-10, sending Bennett crashing off right guard behind Henderson and wall blocking for a 7-yard gain to the 3.

Even from there, on third down, Holmgren resisted the impulse to draw from his tried-and-true collection of red-zone passes and gave the ball to Bennett up the gut.

It would have been a touchdown, too, but Bennett made an uncharacteristic fumble at the 1 that was recovered by Freeman for the score.

After that, Green Bay defensive coordinator Fritz Shurmur played base defense and watched as the 49ers committed four turnovers and gained only 196 total yards.

"Their drive was a sign of what it takes to make a championship team," 49ers coach George Seifert said.

What a mess: Father John Blaha (left) helps clean up some of the Packers' uniforms.

Desmond Howard is embraced by Packers fans after his 71-yard punt return for a touchdown.

Jeffrey Phelps

Fan favorite Reggie White joins in the crowd's celebration after his team's 35–14 victory over the 49ers.

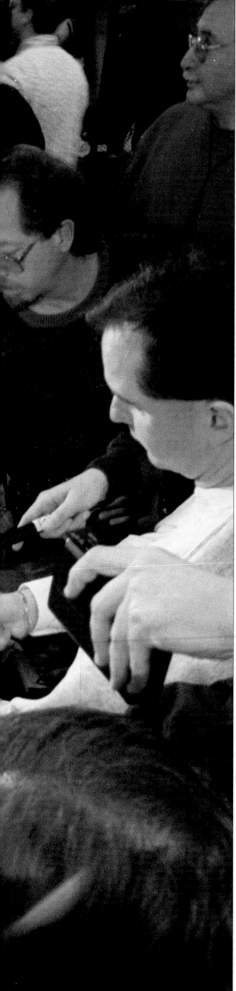

inally, the big moment — the big game — had arrived.
It wouldn't be the long-awaited rematch against Dallas.
Instead the opponent would be the upstart Carolina
Panthers.

Once again, America had fallen in love with the Packers.

The media hyped the contest against Carolina as a football war.

Yet for millions of Packers fans and those who were now
strangely curious about Green Bay folklore, the Carolina game
was only the next step ina journey toward a date with destiny.

Fullback William Henderson, hoping to get away from the media, takes a few
moments to relax and contemplate the task at hand.

Just weeks after receiver Andre Rison
was released by Jacksonville, he
found himself the focus of media
attention leading up to the NFC
Championship game.

On Tuesday, it hardly looked like a championship game would be played at Lambeau Field in a matter of days.

Tom Lynn

Tom Lynn

In a race against Mother Nature, grounds crews rolled out the new turf, which was trucked in to replace the unplayable field from a week before.

Tom Lynn

With the new grass in place, grounds crews added a bit of color to the field.

IF YOU SOD IT THEY W

Home-field advantage includes rabid fans as well as freezing temperatures.

The NFL's plan to completely resod Lambeau Field was only slightly hampered by snowfall.

Fox sideline reporters Howie Long (left) and Ronnie Lott attempt to keep warm while bringing insight to the television audience.

Carolina	7	3	3	0	13
Green Bay	0	17	10	3	30

29-year Drought is Over for Packers

GREEN BAY — It takes the Super Bowl to validate greatness in the NFL.

And that fact will never change.

But after winning 13 games in the regular season, then destroying the San Francisco 49ers on Jan. 4 and the Carolina Panthers, 30-13, on Sunday in the NFC championship game at Lambeau Field, the irrepressible Green Bay Packers are dead on course to thrust themselves onto the list of the more dominant teams of the modern era.

The Packers' final opportunity to leave an indelible impression will come in New Orleans in two weeks when the emerging force from the NFL's smallest city will return to the Super Bowl for the first time in 29 years.

Their opponent in Super Bowl XXXI will be the New England Patriots, 20-6 winners over the Jacksonville Jaguars in the AFC championship game.

"We have a great football team, and we're not finished yet," Packers coach Mike Holmgren said on the field during the raucous presentation of the George S. Halas Trophy, symbolic of the NFC championship.

Some in the crowd of 60,216 at Lambeau Field wept tears of joy, having waited almost three decades for the Packers

to recapture glory after mostly 30 years of largely post-Lombardi mediocrity.

"Not bad, huh?" Packers general manager Ron Wolf said. "A lot of people never thought this was going to happen. They thought this was a dead issue up here in Wisconsin."

But with Wolf procuring the players and Holmgren installing superb systems in a disciplined but sanguine environment, the Packers improved every season since their administration began in 1992.

Today, they are a prohibitive favorite to add the franchise's third Lombardi Trophy.

Packers cornerback Tyrone Williams stretches and pulls in a one-handed interception of a pass intended for Willie Green.

Benny Sieu

Gary Porter

Edgar Bennett is thankful after scoring on a 4-yard touchdown run to give the Packers a 27-13 lead to end the third quarter.

"We're a very good football team," Packers two-time MVP quarterback Brett Favre said. "Everyone expected us to win that ball game today, including ourselves. And we did.

"I'm assuming that people will think we should win the Super Bowl, and we probably should, if statistics and records come into play. But anything can happen."

At least the Patriots won't have to cope with the frigid weather — 3 degrees with a minus-17 windchill at kickoff — and rabid crowds that have turned Lambeau into the league's most overwhelming venue for visitors.

Carolina (13-5) suffered the worst defeat of its storybook season mainly because its quirky zone-blitz defense allowed 479 yards, the most against the Panthers in their two seasons, and the second-highest total by the Packers under Holmgren.

"I would have never guessed we would

One fan wears a telling sign of the frigid conditions at the NFC Championship game. Temperatures dipped to 3 degrees by the kickoff.

Benny Sieu

Reggie White kept pressure on Carolina quarterback Kerry Collins all afternoon.

Jeffrey Phelps

come in here and have our butts handed to us like we did today," Panthers linebacker Kevin Greene said. "Another thing I never would have believed is that a team could run the ball on us like they did.

"They just gashed us here and gashed us there."

After a typically sluggish start, including two turnovers by Favre that led to Carolina's first 10 points, the Packers unleashed the full authority of their offensive might in a startling mix of grind-it-out running and big-play passing.

The West Coast offense, in all of Holmgren's subtle alterations, seldom, if ever, was this unstoppable.

In fact, Green Bay offensive coordinator Sherman Lewis, who won three Super Bowl rings as a 49ers' assistant from 1983-'91, went so far as to say that the Packers' offense is as complete and potent as any he was associated with in San Francisco.

Operating with equal effectiveness from the I-formation against Carolina's base 3-4 defense and with three and four receivers against nickel defenses, the Packers amassed 201 rushing yards against a defense that held Dallas to 85 the week before.

Dale Guldan

A trip to the Super Bowl is more than enough reason for Terry Mickens to let out a victorious yell after the Packers won the NFC Championship game.

This shocking resurgence in rushing has left Green Bay with a 152.2-yard average in its last six games compared with 91.4 yards over the previous nine games.

Dorsey Levens (10 carries, 88 yards) and Edgar Bennett (25-99) have been magnificent. So, too, according to Lewis, has been the lead blocking of fullback William Henderson and an offensive line that seems on a mission to prove its worth.

Wary of Panthers coach Dom Capers' defensive scheme, Holmgren did almost everything on offense except put Favre back seven steps and wing it. Starting with Levens' 35-yard burst on the final play of the first quarter, the Packers struck for seven plays of 20 yards or more.

It was all there for the Panthers to behold and, ultimately, fail to contain: two dangerous tight ends forcing the safeties to stay back, receivers breaking tackles after the catch, running backs moving as fluidly as receivers, screen passes executed in exquisite fashion and a dashing quarterback making it all work.

Despite trailing by 7-0 early and then 10-7 late in the first half, the Packers had no real reason for self-doubt. Despite its many limitations in personnel, Carolina was well-prepared and surprisingly dangerous on offense, but its defense kept guessing wrong and ended up being humiliated.

"Yeah, I felt we'd come back," Favre said. "I don't think anybody can stop us, I really don't."

Carolina, which had outscored opponents, 200-62, in the second half, was in danger of being counted out before Holmgren mercifully quit passing early in the fourth quarter.

"We have a lot of individuals who had awards presented to them but they have a bunch of no-name players with tremendous heart, a great quarterback and a great coach," Panthers linebacker Lamar Lathon said. "We should pattern ourselves after them."

Brett Favre goes down, but not before getting off a shovel pass to Dorsey Levens for a first down.

Jeffrey Phelps

In a situation where the ice might be warmer than the surrounding air, Packers coach Mike Holmgren gets a dousing as the seconds tick away in the NFC Championship game.

Antonio Freeman (left), Don Beebe and Andre Rison shake on it — the Packers are headed to the Super Bowl.

Photo on Pages 140-141 by Dale Guldan

Dale Guldan

The Packers bench erupts as the clock runs down and the players realize that they're going to the Super Bowl.

Sean Jones gives the George Halas Trophy a lift for all of Wisconsin to see.

Favre

GREEN BAY — Gulls drifted aimlessly overhead in the approaching dusk of a hot, humid evening in Tampa, Fla.

The Green Bay Packers had just completed the first leg of their season to end all seasons at Houlihan's Stadium behind the exploits of their spectacular quarterback, a man who knew exactly where he had come from and where he intended to go.

It was Opening Day 1996, Tony Dungy's debut as coach of the Tampa Bay Buccaneers. But the eyes of the football world were trained on one man: Brett Lorenzo Favre.

Just two months earlier, Favre had been released from a treatment center in Kansas after his 46-day stay for an addiction to the painkiller Vicodin.

And after Favre's uneventful exhibition campaign, the NFL eagerly awaited the first sign of whether last season's most valuable player would be the same player in the new year.

Clearly, the Packers' hopes for the Super Bowl rested on his shoulders. He had been their bell cow since arriving via a trade from Atlanta in 1992.

For Favre, the son of a Mississippi high school football coach, leading was a way of life. "Tell me I can't do something and I'll do it," he had said once, and his entire career was about proving that he could beat the odds.

With only Packers fans cheering after the 34-3 rout, Favre walked off the field with Green Bay tight end Mark Chmura, one of his closest friends and someone who had stood beside him when others questioned if Favre's career might spiral out of control in the throes of chemical dependency.

"I said to him, 'Great game,'" Chmura said. "And he said to me, 'I guess the old Brett never left.'"

Tampa Bay was the first of five regular-season games in which Favre would throw four touchdown passes. The Packers dominated the contest, the start of a galvanizing journey in which Favre made good on his promise of "Super Bowl or bust."

That was typical Favre: Out front, alone, unafraid to speak what most or all of his teammates were thinking.

And four months later, after the Packers had won 13 games and their quarterback had passed for the third highest touchdown total in history (39), the ultimate individual award was his.

MVP, once again.

Only Joe Montana, recognized by many as the best quarterback of all time, won the award in back-to-back seasons.

"This is an awful thing to say, because Montana is a legend," San Diego Chargers general manager Bobby Beathard said. "But I don't know that Montana would have been as successful as he was had he been in a traditional pro system.

"However, I think Favre would be as successful in any system. He would be this

Jeffrey Phelps

The short pass is the bread and butter play of the West Coast offense, as Brett Favre demonstrates against the Chiefs.

good in any era."

Sometimes described as a throwback to the days of colorful, swashbuckling quarterbacks such as Bobby Layne, the 27-year-old Favre is on a fast track to the Pro Football Hall of Fame.

Even now, after just six seasons, his career passer rating of 88.6 ranks third on the all-time list behind two other magnificent practitioners of the West Coast offense, the 49ers' Steve Young (96.2) and the old 49ers' icon, Montana (92.3).

"I have never seen a quarterback in this league at his young age who is as good as he is," said Mr. Quarterback himself, Bart Starr. "Coach Lombardi would have loved him."

Not initially. After Ron Wolf and coach Mike Holmgren successfully pried him away from the Falcons for a first-round draft choice, they were slightly unprepared for the raw, unfinished product that went to training camp.

But even then, at a time when Don Majkowski still topped the depth chart and the unbridled backup was firing rocket passes in every direction, Favre's confidence was telling. Without as much of a change in expression he talked of being every bit as good as Dan Marino or John Elway or Troy Aikman once he had the chance to prove it.

Opportunity arose on the third weekend of that 1992 season, when Majkowski was hurt and Favre had to play. With the Cincinnati Bengals leading by six points in the final minute, and with Favre having had all kinds of problems, he cranked up his right arm and just went deep.

That was the start of the Favre legend, the 35-yard touchdown pass that whistled into the outstretched hands of Kitrick Taylor in the corner of the end zone with 13 seconds left that beat the Bengals, 24-23.

Watching how Favre played — up and down, impossible to predict from week to

Favre's ability to make plays while scrambling, as he does here against the Panthers in the NFC title game, is central to his success.

Gary Porter

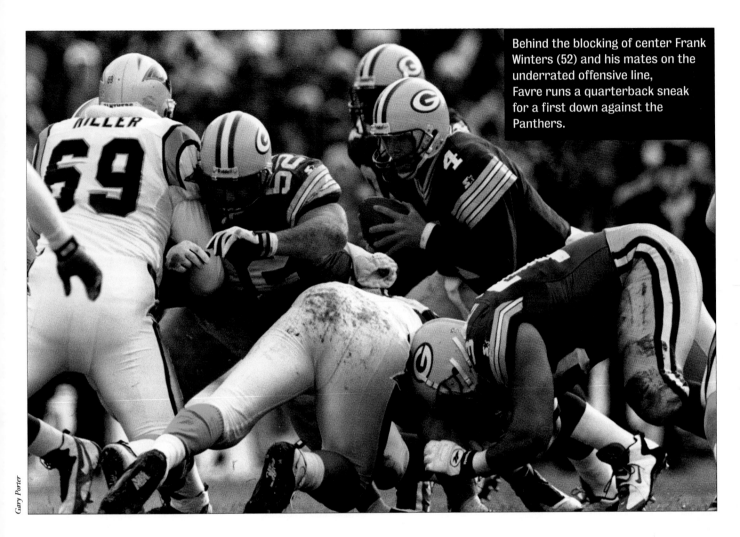

Behind the blocking of center Frank Winters (52) and his mates on the underrated offensive line, Favre runs a quarterback sneak for a first down against the Panthers.

Gary Porter

week — for the remainder of the 1992 season and all of 1993 was relatively easy to explain in the context of a young quarterback's development in an offense that required patience and timing to master and rote memorization to execute.

Under Holmgren, as the 49ers also had done under Bill Walsh, the onus was on the quarterback to control formations, motions and pass protection schemes. It created mental strain for Favre, who probably didn't study as much as he should have early and paid the price with an excessive number of interceptions, fumbles and bonehead plays.

"I've gone back and looked at my report before the draft that year," Holmgren said. "You saw just great talent. Raw ability to throw the ball. I liked him as a person right away.

"I said he throws every pass the same. Hard. I used the term 'blue-collar' in my report. I used the term that he will have to discipline himself in the techniques that we run. I think I was pretty close in my evaluation of him that day."

So the battle between teacher and pupil raged on and on.

Some of the coaches wanted to bench Favre during some games, and more than once it was argued that backup Mark Brunell might be better. Former quarterbacks coach Steve Mariucci reminded Favre so often about curbing his emotions and not trying to win the game on every snap that one of the quarterbacks put a picture of a dead horse in their meeting room.

"He and I will reach the top of the mountain together," Holmgren said in late September 1994, "or we'll be in the Dumpster."

The turning point in Favre's career

Favre and his mud-caked team-mates rejoice after a touchdown in the playoff opener against the San Francisco 49ers.

Jim Gehrz

came about a month later at the Metrodome in Minneapolis, where he played poorly and had to leave early because of a hip injury. The Packers had fallen to 3-4 when Favre returned to his native Kiln, Miss., for the bye weekend and soul-searching conversation with family and friends.

A week later, Favre quarterbacked a near flawless game during a Monday night monsoon at Chicago's Soldier Field. He didn't mishandle the ball even one time, a miraculous performance that to this day represented something of a watershed moment in his career.

"When I got here I would have told you I don't fit the mold for this offense," Favre said. "I was more of an Oakland Raiders kind of quarterback who would complete 48% or 50% of his passes but still have some touchdowns.

"I was totally unsure of whether I could do it because I'd never done it before. I knew my ability was as good or better than anybody else's, but it was a matter of catching up with it mentally."

If Favre's read was clear, he always could deliver the ball on target with incredible velocity. But if the defense was able to create indecision in Favre's mind, often by blitzing or mixing coverages, there were times he would panic and put the ball up for grabs if his primary receiver was taken away.

Simply put, Favre amazed just about every personnel official in the NFL by becoming, as he most assuredly is now, a thinking man's quarterback.

"If No. 87 (Robert Brooks) isn't open, I go to somebody else," Favre said in September 1996. "And if he's not open, I go to somebody else. It's like playing touch football. You can go up and down the field."

And the Packers have, too, finishing sixth in points in 1995 before leading the

NFL with a club-record 456 in 1996.

It was late in the 1995 season when Reggie White referred to Favre as the Packers' most indispensable player, and of course he was right. In December, a Boston writer went so far as to label Favre as "the closest thing to a one-man team since Wilt Chamberlain in Philly."

That might have been a stretch, but consider that the Packers haven't had an offensive lineman make the Pro Bowl since center Larry McCarren in 1983 or a running back who could make yards on his own since John Brockington 10 years before that.

Jeffrey Phelps

Favre has a trainer clean the mud from his cleats in a game against the Bears in December.

Even this season, after Brooks went out with a season-ending knee injury in Week 7 and tight end Mark Chmura and wide receiver Antonio Freeman were lost for a handful of games due to injury, the burden fell on Favre.

Quite clearly, however, those are the situations in which Favre feeds on.

The consummate competitor in the most cut-throat of businesses, he consistently turns adversity into an ally and defies the odds.

"This man has as much courage as anyone I've ever seen," said Starr.

Nothing from a numbers perspective

Favre and Andre Rison celebrate a touchdown pass.

Jeffrey Phelps

Favre stiff-arms a Chiefs defender.

Jeffrey Phelps

gives Favre more satisfaction than his consecutive games streak of 77 in the regular season, easily the longest of any active player and approaching the unofficial NFL record of 116 set by Ron Jaworski from 1977-'84.

Favre's toughness stems from his upbringing, of course, in the brawling bayou country of the Deep South. Another reason is his unquenchable love of the game and the deep obligation that he feels for his teammates to be there for them every Sunday.

"Guys expect the quarterback to get down and dirty for them," Favre said.

"The captain is supposed to be up running the ship, but I think you ain't a captain if you also won't swab the deck."

So Favre throws his body around on scrambles, blocks for reverses and willingly plays in pain. As strange as it was, Favre actually defended Detroit Lions defensive line coach John Teerlinck's kill-the-quarterback philosophy as the best way to coach pass rushing even though league

Tom Lynn

Favre savors a TD pass downfield.

Dale Guldan

2-time MVP Favre has been the center of media attention all season.

"How could I be so dumb?" Favre seems to be saying after tackling Chargers cornerback Willie Clark. Clark recovered a ball that slipped out of Favre's hands on a play that was later ruled a fumble.

Dale Guldan

officials took measures this season to protect quarterbacks.

Invariably after games, one or more opposing defensive players will pay tribute to the fearless and competitive zeal with which Favre comports himself.

"He's an iron man," Packers safety LeRoy Butler said. "He works out every day and is in better shape than any quarterback in the league. He has the strongest arm. And he puts all that together and is still a team guy. He's just a good guy. He doesn't think he's bigger than the team."

Favre possesses almost a sixth sense to avoid pressure, manifested by his ability to pirouette away from tacklers or run up in the pocket at just the perfect moment.

He has great strength and good weight for the position, enabling him to shove aside, bounce off or stiff-arm much bigger men.

He has one of the quickest releases in the game and is the antithesis of a frightened quarterback such as Jim Everett. Sacking Favre takes a real tackle, not a love tap.

And he is a vastly underrated athlete,

with his increasing dedication to year-round training having improved his speed.

Defensive coordinators can't decide how best to stop Favre. Some would argue that it's wisest to contain him because of his extraordinary vision downfield and throwing accuracy on the run. Others watch him pick apart secondaries when pressure is minimal and commit everything they have on forcing him to move from the pocket.

Basically, nothing much works.

Favre has accepted coaching and he has disciplined himself, so if the protection holds up he uses the whole field and distributes the ball to a squadron of receivers. What makes him unique among the great quarterbacks that have directed the West Coast offense is the spontaneity not just to take a gamble but to make it work.

"If Brett were playing for a very, very average team or below average team, he'd still be the type of quarterback that could put them way up in playoff contention," Beathard said. "The Elways can do that. The Marinos can. Now it looks like this guy can, too.

"I can't see any flaws in the guy. He can run and will run. He can throw on the run. He takes chances. And he's developed such consistency."

Wolf, the finding father, put it this way late in the season:

"He's clearly the best player in the league. What the hell are you going to do?"

Savor the moment if you're a Packers fan or someone who admires greatness.

Keep on plotting if you're a defensive coordinator.

After throwing an early interception that led to Carolina's early touchdown, Favre calms down and shows his MVP form.

Rick Wood

Champions!

New England	14	0	7	0	21
Green Bay	10	17	8	0	35

Packers Bomb Pats, Win Super Bowl Title

NEW ORLEANS — The National Football League's version of David stands today as Goliath, towering above the world of professional football.

The Green Bay Packers are Super Bowl champions. ...

Again!

Culminating an amazing five-year rebirth under general manager Ron Wolf and coach Mike Holmgren, the Packers staggered a bit early but rebounded in vintage style to dispatch the game New England Patriots, 35-21, in Super Bowl XXXI Sunday night before 72,301 fans at the Superdome.

"I looked at the faces of my players and coaches and everyone, and I'm just overwhelmed by that," Holmgren said. "It's just a great, great sense of accomplishment.

"We've had a great season. We played a tough schedule. We battled through some injuries. How we compare with other teams, I'm not sure I care."

It was the 13th consecutive victory for the representative of the National Football Conference in the Super Bowl and the

Packers' Dorsey Levens jumps over Patriots defender Corwin Brown, 30, for a five-yard gain during first quarter play.

Dale Guldan

Tom Lynn

Andre Rison hauls in a first quarter pass from Brett Favre as he beat New England defender Otis Smith for the first score of Super Bowl XXXI.

12th league championship for the franchise from the NFL's smallest city.

From the depths of 4-12 in 1991, the Wolf-Holmgren managerial team improved the franchise incrementally season by season until there were no more mountains to climb, just the club's first Super Bowl crown in 29 years to cherish.

Photo on Pages 156-157 by Rick Wood

"The Packers are a great story," Wolf said. "The tradition. The best stadium in the league. The best fans in the league. I believe we do it as well as anyone in the league. We have an identification now."

As a relatively young team with the majority of their standout players under contract for at least one more year, the Packers likely can look forward to being an NFL power broker for the rest of the century.

"Oh, my goodness," Holmgren said when the possibility of a dynasty was broached to him during his understated news conference. "A dynasty in this day and age, I'm not sure if anyone could ever match what that team (the Packers of the 1960s) did.

"But if we can keep our core players together and stay unselfish, maybe we can make a run at it."

By no means was this a dominating effort by the Packers, who had been little short of awesome in blowing out their last seven opponents by a combined margin of 227-72. But after a lull late in the first quarter, when the Patriots pushed across two touchdowns in a span of 30 minutes for a 14-10 lead, it basically was all Green Bay.

"We never had a doubt that we would win this ball game," said Brett Favre, the Packers' most indispensable component.

Once again, the Packers demonstrated that they are a complete, balanced team, perhaps the distinguishing mark of their championship season.

On offense, Favre passed for 246 yards and touchdowns measuring 54 yards to Andre Rison and a Super Bowl-record 81 yards to Antonio Freeman.

After averaging 152.2 yards rushing in the last six games, the Packers found themselves overwhelmed early by the Patriots' speedy corps of linebackers and a

Jeffrey Phelps

Antonio Freeman catches the ball on his way to the longest reception run in Super Bowl history. The touchdown sent the Green Bay fans into a frenzy.

Jeffrey Phelps

respectable defensive line. But as the game wore on, the Packers' offensive line regained their equilibrium, helping Dorsey Levens gain 61 of their 115 yards on the ground.

On defense, the Packers tackled poorly early, which led to the Patriots' first two scores. New England's Drew Bledsoe threw effectively off some wonderful play-action fakes. Patriots wide receiver Terry Glenn was very good, and powerful Ben Coates turned in the most yards by a tight end against the Packers all year with 67 on six catches.

But once again, Green Bay's defense wouldn't be denied.

The Patriots finished with just 257 yards, only 43 rushing in a strange game plan that really didn't even test the Packers on the ground and led to 25 minutes 45 seconds of possession time.

Bledsoe was intercepted four times.

And, on special teams, the Packers thwarted little Dave Meggett while thrusting Desmond Howard into the national limelight.

"Both teams pressured the quarterbacks fairly well," Patriots coach Bill Parcells said. "The difference was special teams. That was the worst we've been outplayed this year."

Howard became the first special-teams player to be named the Super Bowl's most valuable player after he returned four kickoffs for 154 yards and six punts for 90 yards.

"He's as good at what he does as anyone in the league," Wolf said of Howard, his $300,000 free-agent gem who wasn't added to the roster until July 11.

After a 13-3 regular season, the Packers won three games in the playoffs to finish 16-3. With Parcells likely coaching his final game with New England, the Patriots ended at 13-6.

Rison, another one of Wolf's gambles

Packers safety LeRoy Butler sacks Patriots quarterback Drew Bledsoe in the second quarter despite the efforts of Dave Meggett.

Benny Sieu

Packers wide receiver Andre Rison is home free on his way to scoring a first quarter touchdown.

that paid off handsomely, spun cornerback Otis Smith around like a top on the game's second play and turned the move into a 54-yard touchdown pass.

Two plays later, Doug Evans cut in front of Glenn on a sideline route and made a great juggling interception at the New England 28. The Patriots held, and Chris Jacke kicked a 37-yard field goal.

Then the momentum swung completely to New England for the remainder of the first quarter. Keith Byars rambled 32 yards on a screen pass, then Curtis Martin gained 20 on a swing pass.

Green Bay was in good position to escape with only a field goal a few plays later, but Craig Newsome was penalized 26 yards for pass interference on a third-and-10 bomb from Bledsoe to Glenn at the Green Bay 1. The touchdown came on the next play, when Bledsoe passed to Byars off another run fake.

Favre, unsettled and a little discombobulated in the pocket early, was nearly intercepted by nickel back Mike McGruder on third down, and the Packers had to punt.

Back came the Patriots to take the lead,

RIGHT: Reggie White sacks Bledsoe as Packers teammate Sean Jones closes in against the Patriots. This was White's second consecutive sack.

Patriots wide receiver Shawn Jefferson flips over Packers safety Mike Prior during the second quarter.

Jeffrey Phelps

Craig Newsome and Antonio Freeman celebrate Newsome's fourth quarter interception.

Packers cornerback Tyrone Williams breaks up a first quarter pass intended for Shawn Jefferson.

Jeffrey Phelps

with Parcells taking a gamble on third and 1. But his surprising call worked when Bledsoe's play-action pass to Glenn was good for 44 yards to the Green Bay 4, leading to another score.

"That was the best play fake I've ever seen," Packers safety LeRoy Butler said. "They're a great team and had a great game plan. It took the leaders on our team to keep it going. We didn't give up any big plays in the second half, and that was the key."

The Patriots' 14-10 lead stood as the Packers went three-and-out on their next two possessions. Favre had Rison open deep behind Smith but threw a terrible pass that fell incomplete. Tedy Bruschi beat guard Adam Timmerman up the field for a sack. A third-and-6 slant pass for Rison was thrown high and incomplete.

But then, as the second quarter dawned, the Packers regained control.

It started when the Patriots tried to cover Freeman with safety Lawyer Milloy in press coverage at the line, Milloy missed the jam and Favre hit the wide-open Freeman for an 81-yard touchdown, the longest pass in Super Bowl history.

It continued with enormous plays by the defense, including a one-armed sack by Butler on third down and Mike Prior's interception.

Tom Lynn

ABOVE: Desmond Howard outraces the Patriots' Mike McGruder on his way to his third quarter touchdown return.

RIGHT: Antonio Freeman spikes the ball over the goal post after scoring on a touchdown pass in the second quarter.

Desmond Howard jumps into the midst of Packers fans after the Packers won the Super Bowl.

Rick Wood

And it ended with drives measuring 33 and 74 yards that produced 10 points and a 27-14 lead at halftime.

The Packers misfired on their first possession of the second half, when middle linebacker Ted Johnson swooped through to tackle Dorsey Levens for a loss of 7 yards on fourth and 1 at the New England 37.

Then, midway in the third quarter, the Patriots covered 53 yards on seven plays to close to within 27-21. The touchdown came on Martin's 18-yard run through the heart of the Green Bay defense.

Adam Vinatieri's ensuing kick traveled end over end to Howard at the 1. A few seconds later, Howard was prancing and dancing in the end zone, a hero for the Packers with a 99-yard touchdown return and the killer for the Patriots.

It was the first time in NFL playoff history that a player had returned both a punt and a kickoff for touchdowns in the same season. It was the first touchdown on a kickoff return of his five-year NFL career and followed five touchdowns on punt returns: One in the exhibition season,

three in the regular season and one against San Francisco in the divisional playoffs.

The rest, as they say, was academic.

"I think it's time the Lombardi Trophy goes back to Lambeau Field," Packers President Bob Harlan said, making the acceptance from Commissioner Paul Tagliabue, "where it belongs."

Eugene Robinson and LeRoy Butler polish the Lombardi Trophy in the locker-room after the Packers' 35-21 win.

Reggie White cele-
brates, waving the
Lombardi Trophy
high for Packers
fans to enjoy.

Tom Lynn

Packers 1996 stats

The Green Bay Packers, World Champions of the National Football League, and NFC Division champions for the second straight year, finished with a 13-3 record and won the Super Bowl for the first time in 29 years. The Packers boasted an explosive offense and a stingy defense. Green Bay led the league in scoring with a total of 456 points. The defense finished as the top-ranked unit in the NFL and held opponents to a league-low 210 points and an NFL record-low 19 touchdowns. Here's a look at the season by the numbers:

SCORING

	TD-RU-PA-RT	K-PAT	FG	S	PTS.
Jacke	0-0-0-0	51/53	21/27	0	114
Jackson	10-0-10-0			0	60
Levens	10-5-5-0			0	60
Freeman	9-0-9-0			0	54
Beebe	6-0-4-2			0	36
R. Brooks	4-0-4-0			0	24
Bennett	3-2-1-0			0	22
Howard	3-0-0-3			0	18
Favre	2-2-0-0			0	12
Mayes	2-0-2-0			0	12
Mickens	2-0-2-0			0	12
Butler	1-0-0-1			0	6
Evans	1-0-0-1			0	6
Henderson	1-0-1-0			0	6
Koonce	1-0-0-1			0	6
Rison	1-0-1-0			0	6
Team	56-9-39-8	51/53	21/27	1	456
Opponents	19-7-12-0	17/17	25/27	1	210

Two-point conversions: Bennett 2. Team: 2-3. Opponents: 1-2.

INTERCEPTIONS

	NO.	YDS.	AVG.	LONG	TD
E. Robinson	6	107	17.8	39	0
Butler	5	149	29.8	90	1
Evans	5	102	20.4	63	1
Koonce	3	84	28.0	75	1
Newsome	2	22	11.0	20	0
White	1	46	46.0	46	0
Prior	1	7	7.0	7	0
Dowden	1	5	5.0	5	0
Hollinquest	1	2	2.0	2	0
Simmons	1	0	0.0	0	0
Team	26	524	20.2	90	3
Opponents	13	98	7.5	41	0

SACKS

	No.		No.		No.
White	8½	Wilkins	3	Clavelle	½
Butler	6½	Simmons	2½	B. Williams	½
S. Dotson	5½	Gi. Brown	1	**Team**	37
S. Jones	5	McKenzie	1	**Opponents**	40
Evans	3				

FIELD GOALS

	1-19	20-29	30-39	40-49	50+
Jacke	0/0	6/6	9/11	5/9	1/1
Team	0/0	6/6	9/11	5/9	1/1
Opponents	0/0	4/5	9/9	12/13	0/0

PUNTING

	NO.	YDS.	AVG.	NET	IN 20	LONG	BLK
Hentrich	68	2,886	42.4	36.3	28	65	0
Team	68	2,886	42.4	36.3	28	65	0
Opponents	90	3,876	43.1	32.5	15	63	1

PUNT RETURNS

	RET.	FC	YDS.	AVG.	LONG	TD
Howard	58	16	875	15.1	92t	3
Prior	0	1	0	0.0	0	0
Team	58	17	875	15.1	92t	3
Opponents	29	15	237	8.2	26	0

KICKOFF RETURNS

	NO.	YDS.	AVG.	LONG	TD
Howard	22	460	20.9	40	0
Beebe	15	403	26.9	90	1
Levens	5	84	16.8	29	0
Henderson	2	38	19.0	23	0
Freeman	1	16	16.0	16	0
Jervey	1	17	17.0	17	0
Thomason	1	20	20.0	20	0
TEAM	47	1,038	22.1	90	1
Opponents	76	1,649	21.7	45	0

Packers		Opponents
338	Total first downs	248
118	By rushing	74
197	By passing	151
23	By penalty	23
97-219	3rd downs: Made/Att.	74-226
44%	Efficiency	33%
5-11	4th downs: Made/Att.	14-22
45%	Efficiency	64%
1,053-5,535	Offensive plays/Yards	981-4,156
5.3	Average per play	4.2
465-1,838	Rushing plays/Yards	400-1,416
4.0	Average per play	3.5
588-3,697	Passing plays/Yards	581-2,740
6.3	Average per play	4.7
328-548-13	(Comp./att./int.)	283-544-26
40-241	Times sacked/Yards	37-202
3,938	Gross passing yards	2,942
2,437	Total return yards	1,984
26-524	Interception returns	13-98
58-875	Punt returns	29-237

Packers		Opponents
47-1,038	Kickoff returns	76-1,649
68-42.4	Punts/Gross average	90-43.1
0	Had blocked	1
92-714	Penalties/Yards	107-797
24	Total turnovers	39
33-11	Fumbles/lost	25-13
56	Touchdowns	19
9	Rushing	7
39	Passing	12
8	Returns	0
51-53	Extra points	17-17
21-27	Field goals	25-27
31:44	Avg. Time of possession	28:16

SCORE BY PERIODS

	1st	2nd	3rd	4th	OT	PTS
Green Bay	76	125	136	116	3	456
Opponents	32	96	25	57	0	210

1996 REGULAR-SEASON OFFENSIVE STATISTICS

PASSING	ATT.	COMP.	COMP%	YDS.	YDS/ATT	TD	TD%	INT	INT%	LONG	RATING
Favre	543	325	59.9	3,899	7.18	39	7.2	13	2.4	80	95.8
McMahon	4	3	75.0	39	9.75	0	0.0	0	0.0	24	105.2
Hentrich	1	0	0.0	0	0.00	0	0.0	0	0.0	0	39.6
Team	548	328	59.9	3,938	7.19	39	7.1	13	2.4	80	95.7
Opponents	544	283	52.0	2,942	5.41	12	2.2	26	4.8	69	55.4

RUSHING	NO.	YDS.	AVG.	LONG	TD
Bennett	222	899	4.0	23	2
Levens	121	566	4.7	24	5
Favre	49	136	2.8	23	2
Henderson	39	130	3.3	14	0
Jervey	26	106	4.1	12	0
R. Brooks	4	2	0.5	6	0
McMahon	4	-1	-0.2	2	0
Team	465	1838	4.0	24	9
Opponents	400	1416	3.5	37	7

RECEIVING	NO.	YDS.	AVG.	LONG	TD
Freeman	56	933	16.7	51	9
Jackson	40	505	12.6	51	10
Beebe	39	699	17.9	80	4
Levens	31	226	7.3	49	5
Bennett	31	176	5.7	25	1
Chmura	28	370	13.2	29	0
Henderson	27	203	7.5	27	1
R. Brooks	23	344	15.0	38	4
Mickens	18	161	8.9	19	2
Rison	13	135	10.4	22	1
Howard	13	95	7.3	12	0
Mayes	6	46	7.7	12	2
Thomason	3	45	15.0	24	0
Team	328	3,938	12.0	80	39
Opponents	283	2,942	10.4	69	12

1996 REGULAR-SEASON DEFENSIVE STATISTICS

Player	Tackles	Solo	Sacks Assists	INT/ Yards	Fumbles Yards	Recovered	Forced	Passes Defended
Koonce	97	69	28	0.0/0.0	3/84	1	0	5
Butler	88	66	22	6.5/41.5	5/149	1	1	14
B.Williams	83	52	31	0.5/4.5	0/0	3	0	4
E.Robinson	82	56	26	0.0/0.0	6/107	0	0	12
Evans	78	62	16	3.0/25.0	5/102	1	1	15
Newsome	71	61	10	0.0/0.0	2/22	0	1	14
Simmons	67	47	20	2.5/3.0	1/0	0	2	5
Gi.Brown	52	39	13	1.0/4.0	0/0	0	1	1
White	39	30	9	8.5/50.0	1/46	3	3	6
S.Dotson	38	26	12	5.5/30.5	0/0	1	1	6
S.Jones	35	29	6	5.0/28.5	0/0	1	2	1
Prior	29	21	8	0.0/0.0	1/7	0	1	5
T.Williams	25	22	3	0.0/0.0	0/0	0	0	4
Wilkins	19	12	7	3.0/13.5	0/0	0	1	1
Holland	10	9	1	0.0/0.0	0/0	0	0	0
Cox	10	6	4	0.0/0.0	0/0	0	0	0
Harris	8	7	1	0.0/0.0	0/0	0	0	0
McKenzie	6	3	3	1.0/1.0	0/0	0	1	0
Mullen	4	4	0	0.0/0.0	0/0	0	0	0
Hollinquest	3	3	0	0.0/0.0	1/2	0	0	2
Dowden	2	2	0	0.0/0.0	1/5	0	0	1
Clavelle	2	1	1	0.5/2.5	0/0	0	0	0
Kuberski	1	1	0	0.0/0.0	0/0	0	0	0
M.Robinson	1	1	0	0.0/0.0	0/0	0	0	0
R.Brooks	0	0	0	0.0/0.0	0/0	0	1	0

Note: Special teams and miscellaneous tackles not included above.

Touchdowns: Butler 1, 90-yard interception return vs. San Diego (9-15-96); Koonce 1, 75-yard interception return at Minnesota (9-22-96); Evans 1, 32-yard interception return at St. Louis (11-24-96).

Special teams tackles: Harris 21 (14 solo-7 assists); Hollinquest 15 (13-2); T.Williams 12 (9-3); Cox 12 (8-4); Thomason 11 (10-1); Prior 9 (7-2); Jervey 9 (6-3); Evans 6 (6-0); M.Robinson 6 (5-1); Dowden 5 (4-1); McKenzie 5 (2-3); Hentrich 3 (3-0); Mullen 3 (3-0); Chmura 2 (2-0); Hayes 2 (2-0); C.Jones 2 (1-1); B.Brooks 1 (1-0); Beebe 1 (0-1); Mickens 1 (0-1).

Special teams forced fumbles: T.Williams 1 vs. San Diego (9-15-96).

Special teams fumble recoveries: Harris 1, vs. San Diego (9-15-96); Evans 1, vs. Tampa Bay (10-27-96).

Blocked punts: White 1, vs. Tampa Bay (10-27-96).

Miscellaneous tackles: Beebe 2, R.Brooks 2, Bennett 1, E.Dotson 1, Favre 1, Freeman 1, Henderson 1, Mayes 1, Mickens 1, Taylor 1, Timmerman 1.

ENRIQUE RODRIGUEZ/ Packer Plus

The author

Bob McGinn has been covering the Green Bay Packers for 17 years.

From 1979 until 1991, McGinn covered the team for the Green Bay Press-Gazette. In 1991, McGinn joined The Milwaukee Journal as the Packers beat writer. Since 1995, he has covered the team for The Milwaukee Journal Sentinel.

McGinn is a 1974 graduate of the University of Michigan. A native of Escanaba, Mich., McGinn, his wife, Cathy, and their three children live in De Pere, Wis.

The photography

Just as untold behind-the-scenes personnel helped the Green Bay Packers reach New Orleans, so too, has The Milwaukee Journal Sentinel's photo coverage of the Packers spectacular season been a full-team effort.

Beginning with the Gatorade at summer camp in Green Bay, all the way to the champagne in the Superdome, our staff created and handled marvelous images of the 1996-'97 NFL season from a green and gold perspective.

At home and on the road, we shot thousands of images, processed and edited film on site, then electronically scanned and transmitted as many as 45 pictures to Milwaukee for publication in the next morning's paper.

The photo team and five cases of cameras, lenses, computers and scanners were in New Orleans for more than a week. Photo deadlines for daily coverage and this book were met thanks to high speed data lines located in our processing trailer in the photo compound outside the Superdome.

Producing a book wasn't a simple task of gathering the best photos taken during the season. Countless hours were required to select and prepare the pictures for book reproduction on deadlines that would assure the book's appearance in stores only days after the final whistle had been blown on Super Bowl XXXI.

Alan King
Senior Editor, Photography

The Shooters

The names of many of our photojournalists appear in photo credit lines. But, like blockers and the player who sets up the ball for the kicker, credit for a winning season was earned by the entire professional squad.

Mark Gail	Gary Porter
Erwin Gebhard	Jack Orton
Jim Gehrz	Mike Sears
Dale Guldan	Karen Sherlock
Bill Lizdas	Benny Sieu
Tom Lynn	Sarah Tews
William Meyer	Mary Jo Walicki
Ron Overdahl	Rick Wood
Jeffrey Phelps	Joe Koshollek

Picking the Pictures

Picture editors, on location and at The Journal Sentinel office in Milwaukee, looked through the thousands of wonderful images shot to select those that best told the Packers' story.

Mark Hoffman, Photo Editor

John Klein

Ernie Mastroianni

David Trotman-Wilkins

Tom Calteux

Digital Technicans and Photo Lab

Lab technicians spent endless hours sleeving and coding negatives, and making proof sheets. Digital technicians electronically scanned and toned each picture for reproduction.

Digital Techs: Jack Emmrich, Mark Graham, Janine Johnson.

Photo lab Techs: Kevin Eisenhut, Dean E. Johnson, John Watson

Last, but *absolutely* not least, Editorial Assistant Janine Ghelfi organized and maintained a negative filing system that permitted the speedy retrieval of negatives.

Jim Gehrz